Praise for *Drucker on Leadership*

"What Cohen learned as Peter Drucker's student, and their personal relationship afterwards, changed Bill's life. Reading *Drucker on Leadership* will change the way you look at and apply leadership forever."

— Bruce Rosenstein, author of *Living in More Than One World: How Peter Drucker's Wisdom Can Inspire and Transform Your Life*

"Peter F. Drucker helped me found the Peter F. Drucker Academy in China. It is a pleasure to see his concepts and what he instructed me brought together in one place and explained so that they could be applied by any executive. *Drucker on Leadership* is a valuable and useful book."

— Minglo Shao, chairman and CEO of the Bright China Group and founder of the Peter F. Drucker Academy

DRUCKER ON LEADERSHIP

New Lessons from the Father of Modern Management

William A. Cohen

Foreword by Frances Hesselbein

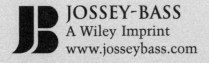

JOSSEY-BASS
A Wiley Imprint
www.josseybass.com

Published by Jossey-Bass
A Wiley Imprint
989 Market Street, San Francisco, CA 94103-1741—www.josseybass.com

Jossey-Bass books and products are available through most bookstores. To contact Jossey-Bass directly call our Customer Care Department within the U.S. at 800-956-7739, outside the U.S. at 317-572-3986, or fax 317-572-4002.

Jossey-Bass also publishes its books in a variety of electronic formats. Some content that appears in print may not be available in electronic books.

Library of Congress Cataloging-in-Publication Data

Cohen, William A.
  Drucker on leadership : new lessons from the father of modern management/William A. Cohen, PhD.
    p. cm.
  Includes index.
    ISBN 978-0-470-40500-0 (hardback)
  1. Leadership. 2. Organization. 3. Management. I. Title.
  HD57.7.C6426 2009
  658.4'092—dc22

                                                              2009029118

Printed in the United States of America
FIRST EDITION
HB Printing   10 9 8 7 6 5 4 3 2 1

For Doris Drucker
The First Lady of the Peter F. Drucker and
Masatoshi Ito Graduate School of Management
but more than that—the author of a best-selling book,
the founder and CEO of a medical device company,
and a woman who not only stood by her man
for almost seventy years
but continues to travel the world
promoting his principles.

■ CONTENTS

Part Three ■ The Military: Drucker's Model Organization

Part Four ■ Motivation and Leadership

Part Five ■ The Marketing Model of Leadership

■ FOREWORD

by Frances Hesselbein

For those who sit at the feet of Peter Drucker, and always will, and for those just discovering our greatest leadership philosopher, *Drucker on Leadership* is a rare and timely gift, as we approach the great celebration of Peter Drucker's hundredth birthday. And who better to bring us this exciting new book, these new observations, than Drucker's first Executive Ph.D. graduate. No one else can claim this unique status—a thirty-year relationship with Peter, a unique understanding of almost a third of Peter Drucker's journey that he shared.

The Peter F. Drucker Foundation for Nonprofit Management was established in 1990. Six weeks after I had left the CEO position at the Girl Scouts of the USA, I found myself the CEO of the new Drucker Foundation. We had ten inspiring years with Peter Drucker as our honorary chairman. He attended our board meetings, three times a year for ten years, spoke at every conference we held, and wrote forewords and chapters for many of our twenty-six books. All of us—board members, staff members, and all—had numerous opportunities to listen to, dialogue with, work on the written and spoken word with Peter Drucker. With gratitude we absorbed and appreciated his messages, his voice, his timeless philosophy.

When Peter became frail, unable to be with us in person, we decided that the most loving and respectful thing we could do was to return his name to the family; we became the Leader to Leader Institute, taking the name of our journal, *Leader to Leader*. But it is the same organization, still committed to moving Peter Drucker's works, his philosophy, his message across all three sectors and around the world. We are as committed today as we were in March 1990 when the Drucker Foundation was born.

I share this preamble to the Introduction with you because my reflections on Bill Cohen's *Drucker on Leadership* have a deep and close appreciation and experience with the hero of the book, and I can say with documented certainty that Cohen's *Drucker on Leadership* is pure Drucker. Every chapter brings a fresh, new approach to understanding the world, the works, the leadership philosophy of Peter Drucker. I read the manuscript with a critical eye, for I felt I owed Bill Cohen an alert if a Drucker concept did not come through clearly or was not consistent with the Peter Drucker that the Girl Scouts of the USA and the Drucker Foundation (Leader to Leader Institute) welcomed, understood, practiced, made their own.

Drucker on Leadership passes this most rigorous test—these lessons are the lessons all those who sat at the feet of Peter Drucker learned, practiced, and lived: the Drucker philosophy. To this day I quote Peter to audiences in all three sectors: for example, "The U.S. Army does the best job of developing leaders, because it develops leaders from within." Bill Cohen's analysis in Part Three captures Peter's respect for the military model of leadership development.

Strategic planning is strengthened by "The best way to predict the future is to create it." We see T-shirts with this wisdom. Peter was the model for the principled, ethical leader. Almost one hundred years of his "gift of example" in leadership and ethics sustains us in our times when far too many have lost their way.

And when it comes to marketing, with "A business has just two functions—marketing and innovation," Peter lights a fire.

In Part One, Bill Cohen is faithful to Peter's focus on "mission," defined as "why we do what we do, our reason for being," which is all about the desired future. Determining what business we are in is a primary responsibility of the leader and the power of inclusion comes through clearly, along with determining who is our customer, an equally powerful message.

Creating an organization's future may seem a formidable task in our uncertain times, when few dare to describe the future—even ten years from now—yet in this book are guidelines for that journey into an uncertain future. Drucker's concepts of the process of creating an organization's future give reassurance to today's planners of the future. When I finished Bill Cohen's book, I felt as though I had been listening to the voice of Peter Drucker himself.

Bill Cohen has been a faithful student, a faithful friend, a faithful disciple, and now with *Drucker on Leadership* he has, and I use a term I learned from Peter, truly "kept the faith."

■ INTRODUCTION
Peter Drucker and Leadership

There is little doubt that Peter Drucker, the "Father of Modern Management," considered leadership *the* essential management skill. As early as 1947, he declared in *Harper's Magazine*, "Management *is* leadership."[1] Seven years later, in his first book devoted entirely to management, he wrote: "Leadership is of utmost importance. Indeed there is no substitute for it."[2] However, despite these clear early statements, Drucker did at times seem to equivocate about leadership. Only a few short sentences after the statement about the importance of leadership, for example, he added, "Leadership cannot be taught or learned."

Clearly, Drucker was ambivalent about leadership—or at least the idea that it could be taught—and he remained so for much of his career. In *Management: Tasks, Responsibilities, Practices*, published in 1973, he reiterated, "There is no substitute for leadership. But management cannot create leaders," and, although the book ran 839 pages, leadership did not appear as a topic in its own right.

Drucker's Evolving Attitudes Toward Leadership

Despite his clear belief in its importance, leadership never became the focus of Drucker's writing. Why this strange conflict?

While we can't know for certain why Drucker was reluctant to tackle leadership head on, we do know that as a young man, Drucker witnessed the rise of Hitler, whose title—*Fuehrer*—means "Leader." That association may well have had lifelong resonance. Drucker himself, sure of what was coming, left Germany almost immediately after Hitler's rise to power. Still, Hitler's success baffled him. Why did so many flock to his leadership? In the end, he concluded, Hitler was a *"misleader."* Misleaders, he said, were "charismatic"—another characteristic of leadership that Drucker had difficulty accepting.

Despite his struggle with the concept, he was well aware that leadership had a critical impact on any project and human endeavor. At the same time, he intuitively recognized that leadership *in itself* was not "good or desirable."

Drucker's conflict with leadership continued well into the 1970s. In those days, I was his doctoral student. I well remember his reaction to a paper on leadership I'd written at his request. He awarded me a high grade, but oddly commented, "Now I'm really confused." For many years, I thought his comment referred to the way in which I had presented my material, since he had not criticized the content. But after many conversations with him, I understood that he was referring to his own intellectual struggle with the notion of leadership during that period. He was still uncertain about leadership as a separate theme, and my ideas, rather than clarifying the issue, probably had the opposite effect.

Yet leadership ran through much of what he wrote. While earlier he believed that the Greek general Xenophon had said all there was to say about leadership more than two thousand years ago in his book *Kyropaidaia*,[3] by the late 1980s he began to realize that he himself had made an enormous contribution to this topic by demonstrating how Xenophon's ideas should be adapted by executives to modern management practice.

It wasn't until 1988, in an article titled "Leadership: More Doing Than Dash," that Drucker gave the word *leadership* prominence.[4] By 1996, he had reversed himself completely. In his foreword to *The Leader of the Future*, he wrote, "Leadership must be learned and *can be* learned."[5] (Italics added.) In 2004, when he wrote *The Daily Drucker* with long-time friend and fellow Claremont professor Joseph A. Maciariello, he abandoned his earliest position. *The Daily Drucker* contains 366 different insights in 72 management categories.

"Leadership" as a separate topic appears more than twice as often as the average of the other topics covered. I believe he gradually came to view even charismatic leadership as neither good nor bad but rather like "the force" in *Star Wars*, with a "dark side" that right-minded leaders needed to avoid.

Toward the end of his career, Peter concluded not only that leadership could be learned but also that it *should be presented* as a topic separate and distinct from management. Unfortunately, he never did this in a book. Jacob High, archivist at the Drucker Institute at Claremont Graduate University who assisted me in my early research into Drucker's beliefs about leadership, noted that the many requests to the Institute relating to "Drucker on leadership" demonstrates the great interest in this topic, as well as its potential value to managers.

While Drucker did not leave us with a unified model of his concepts about effective leadership, I was able to derive the essence of his beliefs from a variety of sources, including his published work—books and articles, oral presentations, and tapes—as well as my own class notes and personal conversations both during my schooling and after my graduation. This book presents a distillation of those resources to give you, the reader, a clear and cohesive presentation of Drucker's views on leadership that, until now, have been widely scattered.

Drucker's Model for Effective Leadership

From my research, I concluded that Drucker believed effective leadership rested on five basic components:

- Strategic planning by the leader as the foundation

- Business ethics and personal integrity as necessary conditions

- Leadership as taught in the military as a baseline model

- Correct perception and application of the psychological principles of motivation

- The marketing model as an effective general approach

The Leader's Role in Strategic Planning

Peter admonished us in class: "You cannot predict the future, but you can create it." More popularly, this is stated as "The best way to predict the future is to create it." Either way, his method of creation was through strategic planning *by the leader*. I emphasize "by the leader" because, although many organizations have strategic planning divisions, the CEO may do little more than sign off on work done by strategic planning professionals.

Peter had a different view. Strategic planning was the first priority of the leader and the leader had to do it. He taught that strategic planning is not about making decisions in the future; decisions can only be made in the present. Therefore, the leader has to make decisions *now* to create a desired future. This implies reaching the stated goals or objectives regardless of later environmental conditions, which would require adjustments and changes along the way.

It was crucial to start with the leader's objectives derived from the definition of the organization's mission: the answer to the question, "What business are we in?" Only then could management decide on the actions they had to take now—in the present—to realize these goals at some time in the future. Part One explores this role.

Business Ethics and Personal Integrity

Drucker was one of the most ethical individuals that I have ever met. If strategic planning was the foundation of leadership, ethics and personal integrity were necessary conditions for leadership effectiveness. In his earliest writings, he stated that leadership was exercised properly only through character, and though followers might forgive a leader much, they would not forgive a lack of integrity.[6]

Peter's views on ethics ran contrary to some of what others taught. He drew distinctions between business ethics and personal integrity. Both were necessary for effective leadership, but he was very cautious of absolute interpretations of "ethical business behavior." He tested many approaches to ethics in his search for a universal ethical code for business, but found them all wanting. In the end, he decided they were inadequate, and settled instead on four Confucian concepts and an ancient Greek physician's admonition as his primary test. Part Two describes Drucker's view of business ethics and personal integrity as necessary conditions for successful leadership.

Modeling Military Leadership

Some may be surprised that I consider modeling military leadership one of Drucker's five components of effective leadership; however, Drucker made many favorable references to the military in class, as well as in his writing. As noted earlier, he believed that the first and best book on leadership was written by Xenophon, a Greek general, almost two and a half millennia ago. Drucker's was not an adaptation of a "business is war" philosophy, but he believed the military model provided good practical leadership. In the article "Leadership: More Doing Than Dash," which appeared in the *Wall Street Journal*, Peter cited Generals Eisenhower, Marshall, and MacArthur, Field Marshal Montgomery, and Julius Caesar as prime examples of effective leadership.

Much later Drucker's view of military leadership received more attention, mainly from Frances Hesselbein in *Hesselbein on Leadership* and *Be, Know, Do*, which she adapted from the official *Army Leadership Manual* and co-authored with General Eric K. Shinseki, a former Army chief of staff recently appointed by Barack Obama to head the Department of Veterans Affairs. Of Hesselbein's adaptation of *Be, Know, Do*, Drucker wrote, "The Army trains and develops more leaders than do all other institutions together—and with a lower casualty rate." Part Three covers the aspects of military leadership

Drucker believed leaders should and should not model, and how best to do it.

The Psychological Principles of Motivation

Drucker was very sensitive to the role and function of the worker. As he saw it, companies were increasingly dependent on the "knowledge worker," a term he created to describe the new workforce whose contributions came from mental rather than manual dexterity. He resented talk of the *cost* of labor and didn't like the notion of *managing* workers either.

To Peter, labor was not an expense; labor was truly added value, a resource, potentially the greatest resource that an organization possessed. Consequently, managers didn't "manage" workers, they led them. This brought Drucker to an unusual conclusion: the best way to motivate employees was to treat regular, paid full-time staff as if they were volunteers. Anything less would result in decreased motivation, making it impossible for knowledge workers to reach their peak performance potential. Part Four examines Drucker's beliefs about how to motivate to get maximum performance.

The Marketing Model and Leadership

Drucker's use of the marketing concept and its application to leadership was one of my biggest surprises when I began my in-depth investigation of Drucker's ideas. I had already concluded that leadership and salesmanship shared the important element of persuasion and had begun looking at literature in both disciplines when Peter published *Management Challenges for the Twenty-First Century*.

In a chapter titled "Management's New Paradigms," he restated many of the ideas he spoke of years earlier in class, including the idea of treating all workers like volunteers. However, in this new book he went further. He called them "partners," and wrote that partners couldn't be ordered—they had to be *persuaded*, and leadership was therefore "a marketing job."[7] What, I asked myself, did Drucker mean by "a marketing job"?

Modern marketing rests on the "marketing concept": the idea that firms should seek to discover and then to satisfy the needs of their customers rather than to concentrate on convincing prospects to purchase existing products or services. In class, Drucker taught that if marketing were done perfectly, selling would be unnecessary.[8] However, to market correctly, the needs of each group or customer segment, including their values and behaviors, had to be understood. Only then could you approach them in the way they preferred and could relate to. In this way, a company would develop products and promote them in the way that the customer—not the marketer—considered important.

By describing leadership as a marketing job, Drucker meant that leaders must know and understand those they wished to lead, and lead in a way followers could relate to. Part Five analyzes Drucker's unique concept as well as my own insights into this initially incongruous-seeming theory.

■ ■ ■

It is unfortunate that Peter Drucker did not write this book. I wish he had. However, using the clues Drucker left, I have attempted to put together his ideas about what we can do to apply what he taught in order to lead with integrity, effectiveness, and honor.

Drucker left us with one of the most profound definitions of leadership ever written:

"Leadership is the lifting of a man's vision to higher sights, the raising of a man's performance to a higher standard, the building of a man's personality beyond its normal limitations."[9]

In this book, I have tried to be true to his definition and to make it my own.

PART ONE

The Leader's Role in Shaping the Organization's Future

Peter admonished us in class: "You cannot predict the future, but you can create it." His method of creation was what we term *strategic planning*—a topic some senior executives ignore as an important element of leadership. Several years ago one CEO of a major corporation called his senior executives together on his ascension to the position and announced: "Gentlemen, I'm dismantling the strategic planning division and ceasing all strategic planning. I am not a believer." Peter, however, was not only a believer, he thought that strategic planning was the foundation of all leadership. In his view, a leader's primary responsibility was to think through the organization's mission clearly and then to promote it throughout the organization, setting goals, priorities, and standards to measure progress along the way.

Peter emphasized that though planning, especially strategic planning, was difficult and risky, it was the first priority of the leader. He told us that strategic planning is not about making decisions in the future, since decisions could only be made now, in the present. So what we were really talking about was making decisions now to create a desired future. The idea was to reach the goals or objectives we set regardless of the environmental conditions we might later encounter, and this would require adjustments and changes along the way. It was crucial to start with the leader's objectives derived from the definition of the mission of the organization, the answer to the question, What business are we in? Only then could we decide on the actions we needed to take now, in the present, to realize these goals in the future. And these actions incorporated the most important task: to anticipate crisis.[1]

All of this had to do with a basic definition he developed for the difference between management and leadership: "Management is about doing things right; leadership is about doing the right things." Only the leader could make the decisions as to what were "the right things," even the right risks to take. Integrate this into a systematic process, and leaders fulfill their primary responsibility through strategic planning. The first five chapters describe what Drucker taught us about how to do this.

CHAPTER 1

The Fundamental Decision
Determining the Business of the Organization

A major responsibility of any leader, according to Peter Drucker, is to determine the *real* business of an organization. I learned this lesson even before I met Drucker and became his student. I was a young manager, but although I had held management and executive titles in several business situations, I knew very little about business management. As a West Point graduate who had served in the Air Force, I knew something about leadership, but I hadn't sufficiently applied those skills to business management.

Shortly before meeting Drucker, I became director of research and development for a small company producing life-support equipment for military aviators as well as commercial airlines. The company was facing increasing difficulties resulting from the government's purchasing policies and timing. My company would receive a contract, and when the work was complete and the product delivered, it would have to wait another year for the next contract. This made planning difficult and resulted in a continuous cycle of peaks and valleys in production, leaving us with too many or too few workers.

About 60 percent of our products went to the government, the remainder to the airlines. We had no product for the individual consumer. About every five years the president would raise this issue and arrive at essentially the same solution: develop a consumer product that would use the same machinery, workers, and materials to smooth out the peaks and valleys. Success would mean an end to this problem. Unfortunately, the result was always the same: initial enthusiasm and high hopes followed by a considerable investment, followed by failure and a big loss. Each failure apparently resulted from a different cause, so no one ever considered there might a larger issue.

One year, at our annual sales meeting, we gave each attendee a copy of Drucker's book, *Management: Tasks, Responsibilities, Practices*. In it, Drucker exhorted managers to determine what business they were in. This subject was number one on the agenda, and it soon became obvious why our efforts to enter the consumer market always failed. The products had nothing to do with our core business of providing life support protection for aviators. For example, we entered the market for protective motorcycle helmets, about which we knew nothing except how to produce the helmet. It turned out that what the military valued and what the consumer valued were entirely different. Furthermore, we had no idea how to reach the motorcycle helmet consumer. In the end, the company invested a million dollars, produced a heavy, very protective but very uncomfortable and high-priced motorcycle helmet that no one wanted, and almost went bankrupt trying to introduce it.

Defining Your Business Is No Small Thing

Drucker taught that determining what business you are in is essential to creating an organization's future, and therefore is any leader's primary responsibility. Once that's determined, a lot falls into place.

An entire set of decisions follow naturally about how to run any organization.

Accurately defining your business automatically saves time, money, and resources that would otherwise be wasted on something that detracts from, rather than adds value to, your business. It also helps you focus on those opportunities and possibilities that are important to building your business. Just as no leader has enough resources to pursue every opportunity or avoid every threat, until you decide what business you are in, your organization will drift, no matter how effective a leader you otherwise are. This is a constant theme in management and leadership: resources of any kind are always limited. Therefore, leaders must make choices and concentrate their always limited resources where they will do the most good. This is true whether yours is a for-profit business, a nonprofit organization, a government agency, or any other organization. Your staff may be striving with all their abilities to support a direction that can hurt your business simply because they don't have a clear understanding of what the real business is or where it should be going.

Today, we call this definition a "mission statement." Drucker's favorite mission statement, though not recent or short, came from a very old business, Sears Roebuck. Simply stated, it was to be the informed and responsible retailer, initially for the American farmer, and later for the American family.[1] It changed Sears from a struggling mail order house, which was sometimes close to bankruptcy, to the world's leading retailer, all within ten years.

How to Obtain Commitment to the Mission Throughout the Organization

Of course, there is only one leader, and ultimately this leader is responsible for the final mission statement and the business. That said, Peter learned much from the Japanese. He had observed an interesting difference in American and Japanese management practices.

American leaders made decisions very quickly but gained little real support for their decisions from leaders at all levels, which caused many of their initiatives to fail.

Japanese leaders made decisions more slowly. This frequently frustrated American leaders negotiating with them. However, once the decision was made, the entire organization was committed to it, and supported it much more than their American counterparts.

Why was this? Drucker found that the Japanese practiced a system known as *ringi*, where all major decisions had to be reviewed and commented on by managers throughout the company. This could require several cycles and months of feedback and revision. However, the consensus built by *ringi* resulted in major commitments by leaders at all levels, who all felt ownership in the decision.

I doubt that adopting *ringi* in all countries would be very effective. During the Japanese management fad of the early 1980s, many U.S. firms tried it. It didn't work. American emphasis on rapid decision making goes back to the frontier days when leaders had to make decisions quickly, and it became ingrained in our culture and the way our leaders operate.

Ideas usually cannot be imported without modification. The cultures and other aspects of leadership and management are different; therefore, that they fail without some modification shouldn't be surprising. Even adopting simple devices may cause problems. For example, traffic signals were invented in England, although the version used today was developed in the United States. Despite their successful use elsewhere, when traffic signals were introduced in Ireland, the Irish were so outraged they actually rioted. Why? Because the red light was on top and the green light on the bottom, and to the Irish, red is the color of Britain; green, Ireland. That red was placed over green was infuriated many Irish people. The solution was to mount the traffic lights horizontally.

Although copying *ringi* in America didn't work either, Drucker recognized the merit of the idea—in particular, the value of consensus for all organizations—and adapted the concept to involve subordinate leaders, but in different ways than the Japanese.

In the past, meetings attended by all managers, or at least those most relevant to the question, were used to garner consensus. Usually someone in or outside the company facilitated the process.

These days, there are many ways to incorporate shared participation in the decision-making process, and these frequently involve new technologies. Glassdoor.com, an online site, allows employees to anonymously review their employers and share salary information. In its annual list of "the naughtiest and nicest chief executives" of 2008 (based on the anonymous reviews), Glassdoor picked Arthur D. Levinson, CEO of Genentech, as the "nicest." He had an amazing 93 percent approval rating. The *New York Times* quoted a strategic planner at Genentech who wrote that Levinson had implemented a decision-making structure that forced authority downward to the lowest possible level in the company, which provided many opportunities to participate and exercise judgment.[2]

Contrary to what some think, general participation in the decision-making process does not make the leader seem weak or ineffective. In fact, an early advocate of this type of approach was the most effective chief of staff the Israeli Army ever had, General Moshe Dayan, the man responsible for victory in two of his country's major wars: the Sinai campaign of 1956 as chief of staff, and the Six-Day War of 1967 as minister of defense. Observers accustomed to directive, high-speed decision-making by military leaders were amazed to see Dayan make some major decisions in his staff meetings by discussion followed by a show of hands!

Why Everyone Should Be Heard

One major reason for listening to everyone as you define your mission statement is to gain commitment. Another, which goes right along with commitment, is that other leaders also have good ideas, and may know something that you do not. By hearing all, you not only gain commitment, you may avoid missing both opportunities and threats to your mission statement. Some executives are reluctant to conduct public meetings about such a major decision, either fearing criticism or that their proposed definition will be defeated. If either happened, your proposal probably should be defeated, or at least modified. As Drucker noted, when making decisions about your business, dissent is a very good thing.

Finally, as Drucker pointed out, the answer to "What is our business?" is never obvious. You need help from others on your team.

Deciding on the central issues of your business or organization with a systematic method in which all key managers participate is essential. With others in your organization focused on the same question, you as leader are far more likely to come up with the answer that makes the best sense and enables you to build your business for the future.

Of course, you need not follow General Dayan's example and settle this issue by a show of hands. The concept can be modified and applied as necessary. Your job is not to sell your preconceived notion but to arrive at an optimal definition of your business through consensus. Do this, and you will not only sharpen the wording of your original definition, you will see everyone in the organization quickly get behind and support the business definition decided upon.

How to Answer the Question, What Is Our Business?

To formulate a definition, you need more than opinions. You must see the business from the customer's point of view. As Drucker wrote, "The customer defines the business."[3] That means certain questions must be asked and answered. Among them:

• Who exactly is the customer?

- Where is the customer located?

- What does the customer buy and why?

- How does the customer define value?[4]

Who Exactly Is Your Customer?

Entrepreneur Joe Cossman started selling garden sprinklers—a flexible plastic hose with holes in it—mainly through supermarkets and similar outlets. One day he read that the poultry business used it to inexpensively cool poultry pens during the hot summer months. He immediately redefined his business and opened an entirely new market for his product.

Many businesses don't track their sales or, if they do, they make little use of the information to analyze and define their business, or redefine it if necessary, and to ensure that both the product itself and how it is sold support the definition of their customer.

Where Is Your Customer Located?

The answer to this question lies primarily in keeping track of sales and the trends associated with them and understanding what they mean. Drucker pointed out that in the 1920s, Sears Roebuck successfully redefined its mission when it identified its customer as the American farmer, and then constructed its catalog—its primary selling tool—according to this definition. Years later (in 1993) Sears quit using the catalog when it saw that the nature of retailing had significantly changed as customers relocated to cities.

It is interesting to note that Aaron Ward at rival Montgomery Ward first introduced the mail order catalog in 1872. It was a single sheet of paper plus a price list. At its height, Montgomery Ward was one of the largest retailers in the country, originally all through the mail. It was said that every farmer owned two books: one was the Holy Bible and the other was the Montgomery Ward catalog. However, times change. Montgomery Ward did not redefine its business until it was too late, and the original business ceased operations completely in 2001–2002—an important cautionary tale of what can happen when a business doesn't know who and where its customer is.[5]

What Does Your Customer Buy and Why?

Some years ago, Falstaff beer, a popular beer in the East, attempted to expand into the lucrative California market. Early attempts failed although blind taste tests confirmed that the brand was exactly what Californians wanted. The error was not in the product but in the advertising, which did not properly promote the *qualities* Californians desired to see associated with their beer.

In the mid-1980s Coca-Cola made a similar and grander mistake on a national level when it attempted to new introduce "New Coke," as a revolutionary soft drink, in response to "The Pepsi Challenge," which was slowly eroding Coke's market. Coke had carefully conducted blind taste tests and formulated a product that was consistently preferred over either its own original product or that of its rival, Pepsi-Cola.

But taste was not why customers bought Coke. Image was. Coke was as much an American icon as mom, apple pie, and John Wayne. Coca-Cola's previous "Real Thing" campaign resonated with this market. America rebelled in mass against "New Coke" which, to them, was not "the Real Thing." Eventually Coke surrendered, dubbed old Coke "Classic Coke," and "New Coke" was quietly withdrawn from the market.

How Does Your Customer Define Value?

Not all customers define value in the same way. What you think may be valued may not be as important to your customer at all. At the same time, you may ignore what the customer really values.

Steve Jobs did a very good job of defining what his customers valued in computing—so good that he and his partners founded an industry. But early on he made a glaring mistake in a computer he called "LISA" by not paying attention to what his potential customers valued. Some said the Lisa was named after his daughter of the same name, although Apple said it was an acronym for Local Integrated Software Architecture. The Lisa had many advanced features, including its graphics. However, at a time when the customer valued price, the Lisa sold for almost $10,000 a shot. Customers flocked to buy—but they bought the competing IBM model, which had less advanced features but was priced much lower. Jobs said customers would buy it anyway despite its high price. They didn't, and eventually even a less advanced but cheaper model was withdrawn from the market and three thousand machines had to be destroyed. It's how your customer defines value that is important.

When Should You Define Your Business?

Most leaders never ask this question, or if they do, it is usually only after they get into trouble, and then it is too late. A smart leader will ask this question when the business is formed and periodically thereafter. Waiting until the situation is critical is somewhat like approaching a doctor only when it is too late for a cure. To spot trends and address them before it becomes too late to take advantage of opportunities or avoid threats, it is wise to ask "What business are we in?" once a year formally, and even more frequently informally and on your own.

Drucker's Advice on Defining the Business of the Organization

- It is a leader's primary responsibility.

- Organizations that failed to do this until too late litter the terrain.

- Make this decision together with other relevant organizational leaders.

- To analyze the business and get to the right answer, first answer the following questions:

  - Who exactly is the customer?
  - Where is the customer located?
  - What does the customer buy and why?
  - How does the customer define value?

CHAPTER 2

The Process
Creating a Strategic Plan

reating an organization's future is an awesome responsibility. I don't remember anyone ever mentioning this when I first studied leadership. We all spoke of the leader's responsibility to accomplish the organization's mission. The future of the organization was just assumed. This is probably true for all of us, regardless of where we first saw leadership practiced. But had you stopped to think about it, which you probably didn't, you would have known this was not automatically true.

We have all seen many organizations stumble, fall, and fail even though they had looked invincible in the recent past. In just about every case, the natural assumption is that this is a result of the tactical decisions made by the organization's leader, helped along perhaps by economic conditions. In some cases, this is true. However, a look at both successful and failed organizations indicates that the seeds of their current state were sown years before, sometimes by leaders long gone.

Drucker's insight that what the organization would become depended greatly on the present leader's actions was revolutionary. It is little wonder that to Drucker determining what an organization was to become was any leader's prime task. How difficult is this prime task? Not too difficult *if* a leader has a methodology. In addition to advice, Drucker had a methodology in mind—strategic planning, but not as many organizations practice it.

Drucker's Vision of Strategic Planning

Drucker's definition of strategic planning was different from most. It was "the continuous process of making present entrepreneurial *(risk-taking) decisions* systematically and with the greatest knowledge of their futurity; organizing systematically the *efforts* needed to carry out these decisions through *organized systematic feedback*" (italics Drucker's).[1] These are the important elements in Drucker's definition:

- It must be a continuous process.

- It involves risk-taking decisions made in the present.

- These decisions should be made with the greatest knowledge available of their futurity—their probable implications.

- The efforts taken to carry out these decisions have to be organized systematically.

- As these efforts are undertaken, feedback also has to be systematically organized.

Implicit in this definition is that a leader is responsible for everything that happens or fails to happen in the organization. Therefore, strategic planning is the responsibility of the leader, not that of a separate strategic planning group. Professional strategic planners can develop plans and make recommendations, but it is the leader's responsibility to give general direction, oversee the process, establish the strategy, direct the implementation, obtain and analyze feedback, and adjust the actions and movement toward the results desired.

This process does not substitute facts for judgment, or as Drucker put it, "substitute science for the manager." What systematic strategic planning does do is strengthen any manager's judgment, leadership, and vision.[2] Therefore, leaders must involve themselves as closely as possible in this process from start to finish.

Although the day-to-day problems of leading any organization cause some leaders to spend less and less time on the critical issue of the organization's future, that is a mistake. It is also a mistake for a leader to establish a separate group to do this planning, periodically "signing off" on the results. There are benefits to be gained from the leader's close involvement that are unattainable through any other means. As Dwight D. Eisenhower, the general responsible for the largest seaborne invasion in history and later president of the United States, said, "Plans are nothing, but planning is everything."[3]

The Function of a Strategic Plan

A plan is more than a combination of objectives, resources, and strategies. It is a road map that will guide you in leading your organization forward to the future you are creating.

The plan shows the route from where you are now to the future you envision based first on the business you defined. It describes the environment you assumed at the time the plan was developed as well as the actions planned. In time, this will all change, including even the answer to the question: What is your business? The only thing certain about the future is that it will be different from the present. However, documenting these environmental variables and your assumptions about them and your business enables you to see the big picture and more easily spot and take advantage of opportunities while avoiding threats.

As you proceed, various issues will arise that could impact your planned strategy and actions. It is virtually certain that almost nothing will go exactly as planned. Your plan will allow you to spot and redirect your activities toward alternate paths to the future you want. This will give you and your successors control and make it possible to take the corrective actions needed to keep your organization on track.

Successful implementation of overall strategies requires integration of many actions, usually by many different individuals inside and outside your organization. It is most important that everyone concerned understand where they are going and why, and what everyone's responsibilities are, as well as how their tasks or actions fit into the overall strategy. In this way, the entire organization and those supporting it can move toward this future together.

Resources to create your future are not unlimited. This is true whether you are an individual entrepreneur attempting to obtain money from a potential investor or you are working in a large corporation and seeking resources for your division. Resources are needed to proceed with your efforts at implementing your decisions. The first questions to ask are

- What resources?

- What will they be used for?

- Why are they necessary?

When you master your plan for the future on paper, you're halfway there. Those who have the resources you need will be more likely to see the potential, making it easier to obtain those resources. As the organization's leader, you are responsible for getting the maximum results from what you have. A well-organized, well-integrated plan will make efficient use of the limited resources available.

Drucker's Three Questions to Determine an Organization's Future

Drucker wrote that a leader must start with three questions to begin planning to create an organization's future:

- What is your business?

- What will it be?

- What should it be?[4]

Although these questions need to be considered separately, they also need to be integrated because the present is connected with the future. You have short-range plans for projects, products, and initiatives. These have an impact on what your business will be in the short term. What should it be relates to the more distant future. How far is up to you. Ten years is not too far. I've seen organizations plan for the creation of a future twenty-five or even fifty years away. Regardless of the time horizon, the answers must fit together. You can't suddenly jump from the business you are in today to something drastically different without taking intermediate steps into the future.

Once you know what business you are in, the task is to look at your present actions and operations to see where they are taking you. Only then can you turn to the final and most important questions:

- What should your business be?

- What is the future you want to create?

- What are the precise objectives of your business in the future?

This is the most important element of the strategic plan because you can't get "there" until you know where "there" is.

Moving Forward on the Strategic Plan

Now that you know where you are going, you need to know how you are going to get there. To do this, you need first to understand the situation. The situational analysis, which contains a vast amount of information, demands taking a good hard look at everything that may impact the environment. Of course, today's environment is good only as your starting point; it is certain to change.

Drucker saw that most planners simply extrapolated the present into the future, assuming that everything would remain the same or that a trend would continue. Of course, this rarely happens. Along the way there can and will be wars, recessions, technological developments, and the sudden collapse of corporations. The only thing you know for certain is things will be different and the environments you operate in will be different.

Unfortunately forecasting for a future environment ten years down the road may have an error rate as high as 70–100 percent. Did you predict the fall of Enron, the attacks on 9/11, or the development and impact of the computer and the Internet on business? Did you predict the onset of the economic crisis in 2008? Even predicting tomorrow's weather, with all our technology and scientific analyses and modeling, is far from 100 percent accurate.

The Impossibility of Accurate Forecasting

Drucker offered a two-part solution to this problem—first, "sloughing off yesterday," and then looking at "what new and different things we have to do and when."

He began with the objectives of the business, and asked: "What do we have to do now to attain our objectives tomorrow?" ("sloughing off yesterday"). He noted that most plans focus on the new: new resource commitments, products, markets, you name it. They never talked about dropping anything. New projects were continually introduced while older failing and marginal projects were continued.

Drucker suggested that a leader look at the situation and ask: If we weren't already committed to this, is this what we would do? And if the answer is no, the next question is simply, How can we get out? Only then did Drucker suggest that the leader proceed to the next question: What new and different things do we have to do, and when?[5]

This wasn't a bad approach. In fact, it was this solution and these questions that Jack Welch, legendary CEO of General Electric, said enabled his huge success at GE. Drucker had asked, "What businesses would GE be in if it weren't already in them today?" Next, "And what are you going to do about it?" Welch said that if they weren't number one or two in a market they would shed the business. According to Welch it was this simple strategy as part of his strategic plan that allowed him to increase GE's net worth by billions of dollars.[6]

Drucker's Secret (Which Violated His Own Rule)

Drucker's famous dictum: "You can't predict the future, but you can create it," downplays any attempt to forecast. However, Drucker himself made predictions, and he was frequently right on the money. He left Germany within days of Hitler coming to power in 1933, a significant fact when so many others held on for years in the vain hope that things would get better. Forty years ago Peter predicted nearly every major change in business that has occurred since, including the impact of information technology and the concepts of the Internet and cyberspace. He coined the term "knowledge worker," and he predicted that these workers would predominate in the workplace of the future. He was the first to view management as a profession and not simply as an activity. He invented management by objectives and more.

Clearly, while much cannot be forecast, some things can be, and Drucker taught others how to do it.

His methods were not based on probabilities. In fact, Drucker said that probabilities were the problem. Traditional planning as done in most corporations used forecasting based on probabilities, even though unique events have no probability. In his opinion such forecasters asked the wrong question. They asked, "What is the likelihood of such and such happening?" The right question, he advised, was "What has already happened that will create the future?"[7] In response to a question from his friend Frances Hesselbein, CEO of the Leader to Leader Institute, about how he did this, he responded that he simply looked out of the window and noted what was going on.

He went further and suggested several questions that businesses need to ask based on looking out the window:

- What do these observed facts mean for your business?

- What changes have occurred that have not yet had full impact?

- What are the trends in the economic and social structure?

- What do they mean for your business?

The answers to these questions reveal opportunities for the future and help define what a company can be as well as the strategies and actions that should be taken to get there.

Drucker's General Directions Lead to New Ideas

Drucker's concept of "nonforecasting" but understanding what effects can be derived from actions that have already occurred led me to adapt some additional ways to further define the opportunities for what a corporation should be and what it should look like in the future. These three concepts are Baseline Assumptions, Delphi Method, and "What If" questions.

Baseline Assumptions

With baseline assumptions, the idea is not to forecast but to assume based on the best information available. These assumptions become the baseline. You can use any methodology you choose to arrive at your baseline. As you implement your strategic plan and measure your progress, you also integrate and update your baseline assumptions so that the environment, trends, and other variables, while still imperfect, are more up to date. Using this data, you can adjust your actions to keep on track for reaching your goals and creating your future.

Delphi Method

The Delphi Method is a structured process for collecting and distilling knowledge from a group of experts using a series of questionnaires with controlled opinion feedback after each question.

In a typical scenario, a question is put to a group of experts on the subject where the forecast is needed. For example, currently the question of when Iran will have developed the capability to produce nuclear weapons generates considerable controversy. Estimates range from a few months to ten years or more. You could assemble a group of experts and a facilitator could ask the question of each expert, who would supply a written answer and justification for it. The facilitator next reads the justifications for each response without identifying the expert and usually without tying the reasons to a particular estimate, and then displays the extreme estimates to the group. Finally, the facilitator initiates another round following the same procedure. After each sequence, the estimate tends to move closer and closer to a single value. In the past, this single value has proved remarkably accurate.

"What If" Questions

"What if" questions define potential problems, opportunities, and threats that might occur in the coming leg of your journey that have a direct bearing on your eventual goals and the new actions taken based on your latest decisions.

- What if an industry you depend on collapses?

- What if you can't get raw materials?

- What if there is a major war?

- What if demand suddenly quadruples?

You don't need to consider every single change with any possibility of occurring—only those most relevant and those with the potential for the greatest impact on your business. For each of these occurrences, problems, opportunities, or threats, you need to decide what you are going to do if it occurs.

Beyond their usefulness in adjusting your plans, these questions can have an important influence on the strategic plans as you develop them. For example, had "what if" questions been asked and acted upon years before the 2008 recession, companies in the housing, financial, and other industries might have made quite different plans resulting in a much different outcome today.

Fine-Tuning and Judging the Future You Have Selected

Drucker had some definite ideas to help you gauge whether your definition of what your organization should be is on the right track. First he stressed that the leader's view of the future must represent what he called "the entrepreneurial view"; that is, a willingness to think in terms of contribution, customer satisfaction, and benefit to the market and the economy.

He believed that leaders must have the courage to make the future happen and that this courage must not be wasted. The decisions taken must meet the test of practicality and operational and economic validity; that is, these decisions *must be actionable* and be *able to produce* real economic results. Finally, Drucker stated that leaders must be personally committed to what they envisioned. In addition, he believed that whatever reaching the future entailed, it must be risky because the one idea about the future that was certain to fail was the riskless idea.[8]

Drucker on the Process of Creating an Organization's Future

- The leader must be in charge of the strategic planning process.

- The process must be continuous, systematic in organization, effort, and feedback, and involve risk.

- Accurate forecasting is impossible; therefore, work to eliminate the no longer useful and to concentrate on the new things that need doing.

- Although you can't make entirely accurate forecasts, you can make useful predictions.

CHAPTER 3

Look, Listen, and Analyze
The Information the Leader Needs

As noted, Drucker said he "looked out the window" to predict the future. Once in class when asked a similar question, he answered, "I listen." After a dramatic pause of a couple of seconds, he added, "to myself." Pressed on this issue, Drucker answered that you had to go one step further and ask yourself what the things you had seen or heard would mean for the future. Thus, leaders need to observe what is going on, and then take the additional step of analyzing this information and deciding what is likely to happen as a result of what has taken place.

Looking Out the Window: A Carefully Chosen Metaphor

On reflection, Drucker's metaphor of looking out the window was not flippant. He recognized that analyzing only internal information—cash flow, liquidity, productivity, competency, resource allocation, and so on—was useful only as a short-term tactic. Drucker knew that strategy of any sort had to be based on information about "markets, customers and noncustomers; about technology in one's own industry and others; about worldwide finance; and about the changing world economy."[1]

In most cases, however, Peter did not say what the information that you should be looking for was, nor in what direction "out the window" you were likely to find what you needed, or even how you might go about analyzing the information. In this chapter, I focus how to apply Peter's advice.

The First Thing You See When You Look Out the Window: The Broad Environment

There are two different ways to look out the window and observe the environment. First, you want to look and take everything in. You will note all sorts of interesting things that are going on, some positive, some negative, and some hopeful, others tragic, some important, others less so. Some recent events provide an example:

In the 2008 U.S. presidential campaign, three major presidential candidates came from three different segments of the population: a senior citizen (John McCain), an African American (Barack Obama), and a woman (Hillary Clinton). In the past, coming from any one of these segments might have been considered a major impediment to election. Of course, only one candidate, Barack Obama, became president. This is a major positive step against unwarranted bias and prejudices, but that would have been true regardless of which candidate had won.

Continuing to scan the environment, we see that the American economy is worse than at any time since the Great Depression of 1929. Beginning with the housing market, everything began to come apart with large, established firms failing, millions thrown out of work, and, at this writing, probably more job losses to come. The economic situation is as bad around the world. Governments fight each other and millions starve in Africa. We are in a "war on terror." There are doubts about exactly how to fight it and even about what would constitute winning it. There are also environmental issues such as global warming, although controversy exists as to the extent of its impact on the environment, and to what extent this impact can be avoided or mitigated.

Truly, there is much to observe out the window. Moreover, any of these events can and will affect the future of your business or organization to varying degrees. These events represent problems, opportunities, and threats. Even negative events can represent opportunities. For example, a relatively weak American dollar has attracted more foreign visitors to the United States for several years, and in lean economic times vacationing Americans may choose to stay in the United States rather than travel abroad.

Keeping Your Focus While Looking Out the Window

With so much to see, you might think that the effort to look out the window would result in information overload. Joe Cossman, the man who sold more than a million ant farms and other products (including the garden hose discussed in Chapter One), said that you needn't worry: when you have a strong interest in a particular subject you will look at things differently and will focus on what you see in terms of your major interest, and ignore the rest.

For example, Joe was always looking for new products to promote. He looked through the window and found that his strong interest in finding new products focused his observations no matter which window he looked through. He saw a small classified advertisement for a solid insect poison, and immediately contacted the inventor, which resulted in phenomenal international sales for a product he called "Fly Cake." At a local fair, he saw the popularity of a rubber ornament in the shape of a shrunken human head designed to hang from a car's rearview mirror. He negotiated the rights and sold 850,000 of these unusual trophies. It seemed that every time he looked through the window, Joe Cossman found a new product.

The Second Thing You See When You Look Out the Window: Specific Targets

Of course, depending on the organization you are leading, you should also focus your attention on what is going on in your area of interest. There are an infinite number of items of potential interest and they are constantly changing. Even trends are important, but sometimes change can occur very rapidly. The ubiquitous slide rule—a tool carried by every practicing engineer in the world—vanished from belts within a year of the introduction of the hand-held electronic calculator. The change was really dramatic—the males wore slide rules like swords and with much the same air while the females kept their slide rules, circular and otherwise, in their purses—then suddenly it was classy not to need one.

The following are a few examples of specific observations that might be of particular interest. While the emphasis here is on customers or buyers, it is important to recognize that all leaders have "buyers" for what they and their organizations offer.

Target Market

You might begin with your target market as it exists. What is your target market today? If you have more than one, what are their locations and their special climatic and geographical features? Are they in a hot, humid environment? A cold, dry one? A desert? Mountainous area? Ocean front? Suburban? Urban? Or what?

Any target market has a buyer. You can categorize each market as consumers or organizational buyers. Organizational buyers buy for their organizations; consumers for their own use. However, depending on the type of organization you lead, "the buyer" may not buy things with money. A politician has target markets. So does a religious leader. Every leader has a target market, and its identity is a critical part of the information you need for strategic planning and for leading.

Cultural, Ethnic, Religious, and Racial Groups

Obviously it would be difficult to succeed by selling food products containing pork to Jewish or Muslim groups. Also, different groups prefer certain types of products. Have you ever heard of peanut soup? In West Africa it is a delicacy. East Asians eat tofu, fermented soybean extract that was once unknown in the United States but has become increasingly popular here for health reasons. You may drink only cow's milk, but others prefer goat's milk. Many Chinese groups drink soybean milk. Among various nationalities insects, monkeys, and dogs are all considered culinary delicacies. Sometimes looking through the window tells you actions to avoid; at other times, you might see opportunities in trends. Always, you see what exists, or what has happened. You must ask: What does this mean?

Social Class

A leader looking through the window might want to observe social class within a certain environment. Social classes are important as segments because people behave differently even though their income levels may be the same.

Some time ago, for example, researchers surveyed three different social groups that had identical incomes. One group consisted of young attorneys just graduating from law school. With their money they bought the best homes they could in prestigious neighborhoods. Naturally, these homes tended to be small. They couldn't afford large homes in prestigious neighborhoods. Next, the researcher called on owners of small businesses whose income was the same as the young attorneys'. They bought the largest homes they could in average neighborhoods. Finally, the researcher looked at workers who had been employed for years by large companies and were making the same income as the small business owners and the young lawyers. This group didn't spend their money on small homes in prestige neighborhoods or larger homes in average ones. Their homes were smaller and in less affluent neighborhoods, but they had better automobiles and household appliances, such as larger television sets, than the other two groups. Remember, all three groups had identical income.

If this research were conducted today, the findings might be different. Yet some variation in buyer behavior among the social classes is still likely. Therefore this segmentation is important, and the identification of the segments that may constitute your target market is very useful information.

Demographics

Demographics describe certain fundamental attributes of your target markets or potential target markets. Is your target market primarily of one particular sex? Are you trying to sell to both sexes or only one? What is the primary age range? How well educated are your prospects? Most products appeal primarily to certain demographic segments that can be defined by answering these questions.

Is your prospect a college graduate? How much money is your prospect making? Certain types of products or services appeal to individuals with certain levels of education or certain levels of income or wealth.

How many people are in the household? Is it headed by a single parent? Male or female? Guardians? How many children are in the family and what are their ages? Are both husband and wife employed? Whether one or both are retired or the family is on welfare is also of interest, since demographic facts may result in different purchasing behavior.

Organizational Buyers and Other "Buyers"

With organizations, you must frequently market to more than one individual. It is critical to know the decision makers and those who influence them. Sometimes these decision makers will include engineers and their supervisors, purchasing agents, and test and quality assurance groups. Each decision maker may have different motivations. This and trends in funding are the most critical factors to observe.

Competitors

Your competition is a critical element. It is an intelligent environmental factor that will act against your interests. Pay particular attention when you are targeting a stagnant or a declining market. If you are targeting the same market segment, your competitor can only succeed by taking "sales" from you. Therefore the more you know about your competition, the better. You should study your competitors, the products they offer, the share of the market they control, and the strategies they follow to help you plan your optimal strategy, which might involve giving your customers better service or a better product.

Technology

In the single year after their introduction, handheld electronic calculators declined in price by more than 50 percent while their performance increased. Computers did the same. You can now carry in your pocket or on your belt an iPhone with more memory than the largest computer of a few years ago, and it has all sorts of additional features. The opposite can also happen. The entire $300 billion vinyl record industry effectively vanished within months after CDs were introduced. The Internet revolutionized the way we conduct business in just a few years and made many competing methods of communication obsolete.

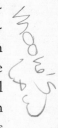

The Economic Environment

I've already noted the economy. It is true that fortunes can be made in both recessions and depressions, as well as in periods of economic well-being. However, the products and services most likely to be successful in these different economic conditions are not the same, and very different strategies may be needed. It is frequently mentioned that more people made money during the Great Depression than lost it. However, success is far from automatic.

The Political Environment

The political environment must be examined because of its potential effect on anything you undertake. There are certain countries to which the U.S. government will not permit you to export, just as there are certain products such as drugs or replicas of branded merchandise from many countries that cannot be imported. The unrestricted export of sophisticated weaponry is prohibited. You must get a special export license, and for certain countries such a license will not be granted. Politics affect the import and the export, as well as the marketing of products and services. It is a part of the environment you cannot ignore, yet these restrictions and laws frequently change.

The Legal and Regulatory Environment

The legal and regulatory environment can cause major headaches. One small company invested more than $100,000 in its development of a new bullet-resistant police helmet. Then it discovered that because of product liability the product could not be sold at a profit. Another firm invested thousands of dollars in a new wine drink assuming that the alcoholic beverage tax would be the same even if they mixed another firm's wine with their fruit juice. It wasn't, and the difference made the product unprofitable. Today, a four-wheeled "motorcycle" popular abroad cannot be sold in the United States. Under our laws a motorcycle has three wheels or less. If it has four wheels, it is considered a passenger automobile and must meet safety standards much stricter than those for motorcycles.

Social and Cultural Environment

Sixty years ago wearing a bikini on a public beach would have been cause for arrest for indecent exposure. Sushi (made with raw fish) has been a popular product in Japan for hundreds of years, yet only a few years ago sushi bars didn't exist in the United States and it was difficult to start one and build a clientele. Today, sushi is extremely popular. Still, some food such as insects, monkeys, and many reptiles or domestic animals may never gain popularity in the United States. In fact, many domestic animals and horses enjoy legal protection from ending up on our dinner plates. At the same time, many countries share a disgust for the mainstays of the U.S. diet.

Market Research: Acquiring the Information You Need

Looking through the window frequently requires research, primary or secondary. Primary research entails interviews, business surveys, and a personal search for the answers. In secondary research you consult other sources such as the Internet. Secondary research is generally preferable because collated information is already available. It should be examined before you spend the time and money to do primary research.

How to Think About a Product That Doesn't Yet Exist

As Drucker noted, getting this information is only part of the issue. In fact, he said that if you do market research and stop, you are heading for trouble. He used the example of the fax machine. The fax machine was an American invention, but was manufactured and marketed to great success by the Japanese because market research convinced an American company that there was no market for it.[2] IBM did the same thing with the personal computer. IBM's market research told its leaders that the market for personal computers was limited to about a thousand a year. This is an almost inevitable result when a product doesn't yet exist. It is difficult for consumers or businesses to feel comfortable paying out hundreds of thousands of dollars to develop a product that doesn't yet exist. In such cases, Drucker suggested that leaders must look at the market—through the window.

How to Determine What Is Likely to Happen

What is *going* to happen as a result of what *has* happened is the other important part of the equation. We know that change is inevitable. But change is caused by events that have already occurred. Drucker suggested that all you need to do is to look at events that have occurred to determine what will happen as a result.

When foreign automobiles first invaded the American market, it was the German Volkswagen about which American car companies were concerned, not the Japanese automakers. In response, Ford introduced the Falcon; Plymouth, the Valiant; and Chevrolet, the Chevette. Americans wanted more than what the bare-bones Volkswagen provided in those days, and, in a few years, the three American models grew in size until they were basically scaled-down versions of their full-sized American cousins. Sales slowly eroded for all three models, which were eventually withdrawn from the market.

All three cars offered essentially the same options, so all three automobile manufacturers looked out the window and saw the same thing. However, one manufacturer looked at what had happened and noted that demand for certain options was increasing even as sales for their vehicle declined. These were bucket seats, "four-in-the-floor" gearshifts, and padded dashboards. Only Ford asked itself what this meant and realized that there was an increasing demand for a sports touring type vehicle. The Mustang was kept under strict security. When it was released, it had tremendous sales to fulfill the demand, easily predicted by "looking out the window" and analyzing events that had already taken place and determining what they meant for the future.

Drucker on the Information the Leader Needs and What to Do with It

- Look out the window and take a good look at your environment.

- Look both at the general and at specific questions relating to your organization.

- Decide what is likely to happen as a result of events that have already occurred.

CHAPTER 4

Methodology
Developing Drucker-Based Strategies

Drucker's views on strategy were quite different from those taught by others. He did not believe in using "portfolio management" or quantitative methods for developing strategy. He never taught such methods in the classroom and a review of his published writings reveals little along these lines. Drucker believed that it was important to approach every situation individually, with common sense and a sense of history. Drucker, although a self-proclaimed "non-historian," used historical examples to illustrate his concepts.

The origin of the word *strategy* is the Greek *strategos*, defined as the art of the general. Although Peter admired the military for many reasons, including its ability to develop good leaders, he did not believe that "business is war" or that one should look at business as warfare. He certainly did not believe in mimicking military principles of strategy. In fact, at one time he was opposed to the very use of the word *strategy* in business because he thought it was too closely associated with the military and might lead business leaders astray in their approach to strategy development.[1] Nevertheless, he recognized that there were common strategic principles that organizations shared with the military.

For example, the military or any organization operates on a "theory of business."[2] Drucker wrote that strategy converted this theory of business into performance; that its purpose was to enable an organization to achieve its desired results in an unpredictable environment.[3] He distinguished planning from the strategy involved; according to Drucker planning tries to optimize tomorrow the trends of today, while strategy seeks to exploit the new and different opportunities of tomorrow.[4] I have elected not to distinguish planning in this way, because strategic planning as I have defined it here may or may not incorporate trends and because both strategy and planning should seek to exploit new and different opportunities lying in the future.

Strategy Not by Formula

Drucker's aversion to "portfolio management" included the well-known four-cell matrix, with its division into problem children, stars, cash cows, and dogs. It also included the nine-cell matrix developed by General Electric with the McKinsey Consulting Company, as well as other methods based on quantitative analysis and fixed methodologies.

For the most part, Peter's view has been proven correct. For example, in the early four-cell matrix, bigness was supposed to lead to increased profitability through efficiencies of size. In fact, plenty of smaller companies were quite profitable, while some giant corporations stumbled and choked on too much acquisition in their attempt to build. Frequently their bloated size did not allow for a transfer of advantages enjoyed by the acquiring organization to those acquired, which resulted in a loss of efficiency and subsequent inability to satisfy the customer. Many companies didn't figure this out until the 1980s, and for many it was too late.

Drucker's View of Strategy

Peter first looked at a company's overall objectives and whether they matched the business the company was in, what the business should be, who the customer was, what the customer valued and wanted, and what the customer termed successful in fulfilling this want. He would examine whether the organization had gathered sufficient information and if it had given thought to the meaning that events in the environment had for that business. Peter called these "certainties." Pleasant or unpleasant, the certainties had to be faced squarely.

Increasing global competition was a certainty of which Peter was very much aware. He foresaw the likely shift to foreign automobiles long before it happened. He and Detroit knew as early as the late 1950s that overseas competitors were acquiring the capability to produce high-quality, low-cost cars. As quality increased, and with the right marketing, this would inevitably lead to their capturing a dominant share of the American market. Any leader could see this by looking out the window and analyzing the likely results from events that had already occurred.

Drucker knew that American automobile manufacturers would lose much of their market unless they implemented a new strategy. Unfortunately, they did not do so. The oil crisis of the 1970s and the fact that foreign cars, especially Japanese cars, were far more fuel-efficient than American cars only speeded a process already under way. Japanese companies would still have taken significant shares from the American companies even without the crisis. Of course, the importance of fuel efficiency might have been predicted from an analysis of our dependency on foreign oil, something the automobile companies could do little to control. Thus, while the automobile manufacturers might rightly claim that they were simply responding to customer demands in manufacturing less fuel-efficient vehicles when gasoline again became more readily available, they were playing a tactical game that was inevitably going to hurt them strategically, and it did.

Of course, any strategy is risky.

Drucker knew that risk was unavoidable. In fact, he believed so firmly that risk was a requirement for future success that the lack of risk was a litmus test to him. Little or no risk meant that the corporation was not aiming high enough. Moreover, there were uncertainties in every situation, and the future was unknown; initiative was needed to create one's own future. Therefore, leaders had to plan and then take action to achieve the goals they had established. Of course major threats should be identified along with alternatives should these threats become reality. American auto companies could have planned for stiffer competition from all foreign cars, not just those coming from Japan, but they did not. In any case, Peter started with an analysis of the situation in the marketplace and identifying those certainties that would need to be faced.

Questions Any Company's Strategy Must Answer

Drucker recognized that any company's strategy had to incorporate the answers to four questions:

- What opportunities does it want to pursue and what risks is it willing and able to accept?

- What is the scope and structure of its strategy, including the right balance among such aspects as specialization, diversification, and integration?

- What are the acceptable trade-offs between time and money and between in-house execution as opposed to merger, acquisition, joint venture, or other external means to reach its objectives and attain its goals?

- What organizational structure is appropriate to its economic realities, opportunities, and performance expectations?[5]

This recognition led Drucker to a methodology that was more inferred than spelled out in a "by the numbers" process.

A Hypothetical Drucker Methodology

Since Drucker never revealed his methodology for developing strategy as a step-by-step process, I set out to do this some years ago. I researched not only his work but also strategists and strategic thinkers spanning more than seven thousand years of history, from both East and West, and representing a wide variety of fields.[6] I realized that what Drucker did was to integrate goals and objectives (what the business should be) with the variables of the situation and the resources needed along with his judgment based on his own observations. At the same time, I knew his judgment involved many principles of strategy he had not written about, and that he might not have been aware that he was applying in formulating strategies he recommended.

I was familiar with various principles of strategy from my military background and education, but understood that strategy in other areas, such as business, was probably not identical. I was seeking general principles that were applicable to any human endeavor.

At first, I identified several hundred principles of strategy, which I reduced to fourteen. As I reexamined them I found that some of these principles were too specific to certain situations. Others needed rework for clarity and emphasis. Eventually, I reduced my original list again, this time to ten essential principles. They were a distillation of the thinking of many strategists in many areas of human activity, and were applicable across the board to all areas of human endeavor—including, of course, business.

I did not get the opportunity, for various reasons including both our schedules and his declining health, to share these strategy principles with Peter before they were published.[7] As a result, while I am confident of the other parts of the methodology as being consistent with his thinking, I cannot say whether he would have agreed with the principles of strategy that I developed. Nevertheless, following are the ten principles:

1. Commit fully to a definite objective.

   Drucker made it clear that the definite objective was what the business should be. This is why he devoted so much importance to defining this issue. For many years, I have said that you can't get to where you are going until you know where that is.

   The other components of this principle are equally important. The objective must be precisely defined, and must be fully committed to. This commitment is not only important for the leader, it is important to gain and maintain the commitment of those you lead. No one will be more committed than you are.

2. Seize the initiative and keep it.

   There are many stories about individuals who have a great idea but delay in developing it or bringing it to market. Maybe they never do, and someone else does and is highly successful; or maybe they do, but someone else gets in just a little bit sooner. This principle says you must get the initiative and keep it until you achieve your goal. Drucker emphasized action. It's not enough to have a great idea—you must take action on it for it to mean anything.

3. Economize to mass your resources.

   You can't be strong everywhere because your resources will always be limited. Consider time. We all get the same amount, but some waste a good deal and spend it in areas unrelated to the goals they seek. The idea is to economize where your efforts and resources are not critical and concentrate them where they are more important. You must concentrate superior resources at the decisive point in the situation. This is exactly what Drucker was saying when he asked Jack Welch his two famous questions (see Chapter Two).

4. Use strategic positioning.

To achieve any strategic objective, you will need to maneuver due to environmental or other unexpected changes. You may need to modify your approach and your positioning, even as you continue to work toward an objective. If what you are doing isn't working, you need to alter your strategy. Although persistence is an immensely valuable trait for reaching any goal, maintaining a faulty strategy in pursuit of a goal is foolish or worse.

5. Do the unexpected.

Surprising your competition by doing the unexpected is very effective. Similarly, this principle can be profitably applied to your customers, as long as the surprise is pleasant. It goes along with the concept of giving your customers more than they expect.

6. Keep things simple.

Someone at NASA once calculated that if every single one of the parts in one of NASA's rockets were 99.9 percent reliable, the rocket would fail 50 percent of the time. The more things that can go wrong, the more will go wrong. If you want less to go wrong, keep your strategy simple.

7. Prepare multiple simultaneous alternatives.

Since some actions are going to fail, you should always have an alternative action thought through and ready to be implemented.

8. Take the indirect route to your objective.

Moving directly against any entrenched human thought or endeavor always arouses opposition. No one likes to be sold anything. However, most are eager to take advantage of a bargain. The difference is subtle, but the results can be decisive. The direct route always leads to the strongest opposition. The same principle holds true in a situation where there is competition that must be faced, and this principle should be integrated into your strategy. This concept was first explained fully by B. H. Liddell Hart, probably the greatest strategist of the last century, whose book, *Strategy*, first published more than fifty years ago, is still in print.[8]

9. Practice timing and sequencing.

   Implementing the "right" strategy at the wrong time or in the wrong sequence can be as ineffective as implementing the wrong strategy. You may have heard someone say, "He was ahead of his time," meaning that someone with the same idea at the "right" time was extraordinarily successful. Bottled water in the United States is very successful today, and some branded names command very high prices. Yet fifty years ago, the idea of paying for water would have been a joke.

10. Exploit your success.

    Don't stop or slow down when you are achieving your objectives. Not staying ahead of your competition is simply giving them another chance to stop you.

Principles, Resources, and Fixed Certainties

To develop strategy, Drucker saw that three elements—the principles of strategy, the resources of the firm, and what he called the "fixed certainties"—needed to be brought together. The organization of his methodology was also employed by an earlier strategist, the Englishman J.F.C. Fuller.[9]

After deciding what the business should be, the leader looks at all aspects of the situation to carefully select the relevant certainties, which must be turned to advantage, avoided, overcome, or ignored. The strategist's purpose is to integrate the relevant variables with the principles, and using the available resources, develop a plan to accomplish the mission.

Table 4.1 lists these three aspects side by side. Rather than relying on numbers, statistics, percentages, and the like, this chart provides a quick overview of the elements that should be considered when developing an appropriate strategy for a given situation.

Table 4.1—Elements of a Strategy

Drucker's Fixed Certainties	Principles	Available Resources
Economic conditions	Commitment to a definite objective	Manpower
Business conditions	Seizing and maintaining the initiative	Capital
State of technology	Economization to mass	Equipment
Politics	Positioning	Special knowledge
Legal and regulatory issues	Surprise	Leaders
Social and cultural norms	Simplicity	Other relevant resources
The competition	Multiple simultaneous alternatives	
Other relevant variables	The indirect approach Timing and sequencing Exploitation of success	

Developing Strategy Based on Drucker's Concepts

- Decide what business you are in and what the business should be.

- Initiate the process of creating the organization's future.

- Get the information you need and determine what the effect of earlier events will mean.

- Bring together the fixed certainties, the resources required, and the principles of strategy.

- Decide on action steps to implement the strategy.

- Take action.

CHAPTER 5

Taking Action
What It Takes to Implement Your Plan

eter Drucker was a man of action. He wrote that the best plan is only a plan, mere good intentions unless it generates work.[1]

His preference for action and the application of knowledge over the theoretical and the academic cost him favor with some academics. However, this same focus is what led practitioners to acclaim his ideas, and even his academic detractors acknowledged him as the "Father of Modern Management."

Without action, nothing is achieved and nothing is accomplished. Without action, your strategic planning is worthless because you won't be able to implement this very basic responsibility of the leader.

How many very talented leaders have you known who excelled in almost every department except one—the ability to "follow through." This doesn't necessarily mean that they failed to initiate the action their plans required. It means that this is all they did. They turned the switch on and stopped with that. There was no updating or oversight; they did not attempt to make sure the actions they had initiated were carried out. They did not attempt to discover whether everything was working out as intended or the organization's future was being shaped as they had envisioned or anything should be changed or fine-tuned. In failing the critical task of follow-through, they wasted the time, effort, and resources of everyone involved.

In this chapter, I discuss how you can organize and implement Drucker's advice in executing your plans to build your organization, whatever its mission, into what it should be. Your objective is not a beautifully leather-bound, well-organized and worded document that rests quietly on your office bookshelf, taken down only to be shown off to visitors. Your objective—and the only one worth talking about—is to make your organization what it should be.

Implementing and Controlling Your Plan

Implementing your plan means initiating and putting your plans into action. As with any project, your strategic plan needs leadership and management. This requires that tasks be broken down, assigned, and scheduled. Resources must be allocated, and performance expectations defined, and metrics established, and a system for periodic and ad hoc reviews and feedback implemented. In short, as leader you are responsible for and must implement the plan.

To do this, a leader needs controls, which according to Drucker have three major characteristics.[2] They

- Can be neither objective nor neutral.

- Need to focus on results.

- Must consider measurable and nonmeasurable events.

Controls Can Be Neither Objective Nor Neutral

No matter how scientific you are, when you control something you induce error in measurement. Since it is essential to measure the effect of strategy, this is important because the very act of establishing the control creates focus and can influence results.[3]

The most famous (or infamous) example of errors that controls can induce was a study done at the Hawthorne Works in Cicero, Illinois, beginning about 1924. An experiment was set up to measure productivity improvement that resulted from improved illumination of the work area. Not surprisingly, researchers found that when they increased the light bulb's wattage, worker productivity increased. However, productivity continued to improve even though the wattage was increased only slightly. Suspicious, the investigators decreased the wattage. Surprise, surprise, productivity still increased! The fact that attention was being paid to the workers during the experiments caused a short-term increase in productivity.

This became known as the Hawthorne Effect, and it has been observed many times in different settings and environments, although it is still controversial, as it has not always been replicated.[4] Still, there is enough evidence to support Drucker's assertion as a cautionary note. The basic question then is what exactly is it that should be measured and controlled?[5]

Controls Must Focus on Results

Drucker noted that the major difference between a manager and a leader is that the manager focuses on doing things right, while the leader focuses on doing the right things. This is not a simple play on words. Of course you would like a leader who is both efficient (doing things right) and effective (doing the right things), but if it is a choice between the two, and this determines focus, then the leader must focus on getting the right job done, at the expense of efficiency.

This was the great weakness of the Total Quality Management (TQM) movement, which had many good attributes including ownership, continuous improvement, empowerment, and, of course, its goal of quality. However, TQM specifically focused on process rather than results. The theory was that if you had the most efficient process in place then the best result would naturally follow. Unfortunately, this was not necessarily true. The Florida Power and Light Company (winner of Japan's Deming Prize for quality management) abandoned TQM within a year due to worker complaints, while the Wallace Company, a Houston oil supplier, won the prestigious Malcolm Baldrige National Quality Award and promptly went bankrupt.[6] The point is that the control system you implement must focus on your goals, and not on gaining efficiencies along the way.

Both Measurable and Nonmeasurable Events Need Controls

According to Drucker, it is possible and important to control both measurable and nonmeasurable events. His concern was that obviously measurable events would gradually overshadow nonmeasurable results, which were frequently more important. In the context of a strategic plan, most if not all events are measurable or can be made so. Drucker's example of a critical nonmeasurable event was an organization's need to attract and hold able employees.[7] While the *need* to attract and hold able employees may not be measurable, measurements can be designed to calculate how an organization is doing in meeting this need. These might measure employee satisfaction, turnover rates, time to acquire new hires, and so forth.

Drucker's Metrics for Control

Both choosing the correct metrics and making the correct decisions about them are incredibly important to achieving any goal whether strategic or everyday. Choice of the wrong metrics or application of incorrect data collection or analysis can lead to a multitude of problems for the organization—in addition to failing in the basic control function.

A large Air Force command established a management control system and developed performance measurements to control important aspects of the organization's primary mission and support functions. One of the support functions at most U.S. military installations consists of social club-like organizations, which can be very simple, or for the larger permanent bases, quite elaborate. In this command, as is often the case, all were for the benefit of all ranks, their families and guests, and were supported by the membership, not the government. Membership was voluntary, although there was some pressure to participate; therefore, almost all joined and paid a modest monthly membership fee. Since club membership fees were kept very low, a disproportionate amount of income came from the bars, which tended to make the entire club profitable, although they were not set up to be profit centers.

The higher organizational level decided that the basic metric for all clubs would be profits, but not just overall profit, profit in each part of the club. The new management control system created immediate problems. The swimming pools now had to charge a fee. Use declined. The restaurants lowered the quality of food or service, making themselves uncompetitive with many nearby restaurants not on the Air Force base. Out of desperation and in an attempt to become profitable, some clubs turned to highly questionable cost-cutting practices. One club stopped purchasing catsup and mustard bottles. Instead, the unused government-issue tubes were salvaged from flight lunch boxes. Members deserted the club restaurants and soon membership declined. Only when metrics based on service as well as profits were introduced did the clubs return to their previous state.

Drucker's Seven Specifications

Because of the importance of metrics in establishing controls, Drucker created seven specifications for effective control.[8]

First, a control must be economical to both managers and the leader. When Frank Carlucci was secretary of defense, I heard him speak about his early experiences in this cabinet position. He oversaw several million employees in and out of uniform and billions of dollars in defense expenditures. To control such a vast empire, he required a great deal of information from the many defense organizations under his supervision. His staff put together a list of the information they thought that he would need from each. Carlucci asked each organization to collect, analyze, and present the results to him during a personal visit, which he intended to make every six months. Six months later, on his first visit, he received an immense document. Pleased, he said that this was exactly what he wanted. Later, he learned that in order to obtain all the information required by him every six months, the organization would have to spend most of its time and a huge amount of resources on this one task and not on performing its mission. After his staff reviewed the requirements with this in mind, he found that a tiny percentage of the information originally requested was all he needed for effective control and oversight.

Second, Drucker found that many organizations measured things that were unimportant to the leader's intended outcome, and were therefore meaningless. If a control is not meaningful, you are not only wasting time and effort in gathering data and analyzing it, you will be sending the wrong signals to subordinates as your organization proceeds with the plan. Those you lead will waste time, energy, and resources working on the wrong objectives. The control must be meaningful to your ultimate objective for your strategic plan.

Third—the most important specification—the control must be appropriate to what is being measured. He found that many controls supplied numbers without a description that defined what the numbers meant. For example, sales performance is frequently reported in total dollars, which by itself is inappropriate because an identical volume of sales could mean substantial profit, zero profit, or a substantial loss, depending on the product mix.

Fourth, measurements must be compatible with the events being measured. He warned of the tyranny of numbers and cautioned that frequently an exact number, although it seemed precise, could be so inaccurate as to be meaningless—even dangerous—because its implied certainty misled leaders about the real nature of the event. Terms such as "larger," "smaller," "earlier," and "later" were often more accurate than numbers. For example, deliveries described as being on average only 1.2 days late might in fact have been half late by a week and half early by almost the same amount.

Fifth, measurements should be taken at appropriate intervals. The tendency, Drucker reported, is to assume frequent measurement and feedback are essential. However, frequency is not always required, nor is early reporting. As Secretary Carlucci discovered, measurements and control have a cost; frequency increases that cost and, if unnecessary, can be counterproductive. The key is to make the control timely. Not too frequent or too infrequent, and not too early or too late, but timed to the thing being measured and the need for immediacy.

Sixth, make controls as simple as possible. Complicated controls and rules confuse—and it's true, as Murphy's Law says, that "everything that can go wrong, will go wrong." Complex controls make measurement more difficult and costly, and they induce a greater chance of error.

Seventh, make all controls "operational." By this, Drucker meant that the results sought should lead to action, not merely be of interest or "academic."

The Importance of Periodic Reviews

Based on the feedback from the controls, the leader may adjust strategy, goals, and objectives, or even reinvent everything as the organization is guided continually toward what it should become. If the environment changes suddenly, even the purpose of the organization may need to be adjusted rapidly, perhaps immediately, for the sake of survival.

Drucker recognized that reorganization was "major surgery." Still, that's what slide rule, vinyl record, and railroad companies should have done. To maintain control, strategic planning review should be done periodically, probably annually, and ad hoc reviews should occur whenever a major opportunity or threat occurs or a "certainty" in the equation is no longer certain. These reviews may involve anything from fine-tuning to reinventing the organization from the top down and bottom up.

The Ultimate Control

Drucker recognized that the ultimate control was the fact that people act according to the metrics because they know rewards and punishments will be dispensed based on them.[9] So even the carrot-and-stick approach, which Drucker did not usually recommend, had a place. In the example of the military clubs, one of the dysfunctions was that the profit metrics established focused subordinate leaders on profits rather than service, which was the original intent. A system of control that does not conform to the organization's progress from what it is to what it should be will create conflict and push the organization out of control.

Drucker's Concepts on Taking Action

- No matter how good the plan, there is no progress toward a desired future without action.

- Action requires control.

- Control is possible only through metrics.

- All metrics must meet Drucker's seven specifications.

- Both periodical and ad hoc reviews are required.

- The ultimate control is that the metrics will correctly be seen as the measure for reward and punishment.

PART TWO

Ethics and Personal Integrity

Drucker was one of the most ethical individuals I have ever met. He saw strategic planning as the foundation of leadership for all organizations and ethics and personal integrity as necessary conditions for successfully building on this foundation. In his earliest writings on the subject, he stated that leadership was exercised through character, and though followers might forgive a leader much, they would not forgive a lack of integrity.[1]

However, Peter's views on ethics were different and ran contrary to much of what others taught. He distinguished between business ethics and personal integrity, and, although he believed both were necessary for effective leadership, he was very cautious of absolute interpretations of how "ethical business behavior," a precise term he created, was defined.

At times he seemed to support the view of seventeenth-century physicist, mathematician, and philosopher Blaise Pascal: "There are truths on this side of the Pyrenees, which are falsehoods on the other." He recognized that what one culture might find acceptable or even required for ethical behavior might be unacceptable and even unethical in another. Yet he did not agree with "situational ethics" and warned against them.

Drucker also believed social responsibility was a part of a leader's ethical behavior, but cautioned that under certain conditions what was considered a corporation's social responsibility should *not* be undertaken and was unethical. Drucker's positions on ethics for leaders may be argued, but they must be understood. They form the basis of his ideas about leadership.

CHAPTER 6

Drucker's Views on Business Ethics

Drucker, personally, was extremely ethical in his outlook and all he did. However, both his writing and classroom lectures make it clear that he struggled mightily to arrive at basic ethical principles, which, he believed, were an absolute requirement of all organizational leaders, and his study of leadership led him to the conclusion that while followers would forgive a leader much, they would not forgive lack of integrity.

The Concepts of Integrity, Ethics, Morality, Honor, and the Law

The concepts of integrity, ethics, morality, and honor are closely related, but they are not the same. Integrity means adherence to a moral code as well as to standards of ethics and moral values. Ethics in the context of leadership has to do with rules or standards governing the conduct of an individual or members of a profession. Morality concerns conformity to the rules of right conduct. Drucker defined honor as demonstrable integrity and honesty, adding that an honorable man stood by his principles.[1] All of Drucker's books contain evidence of considerable concern with these concepts.[2]

However, Drucker made an important distinction between these concepts and the law, which may have very little to do with any concept of ethics. He made it clear that the law and ethics are not the same and gave us two examples. Until the 1860s, slavery was legal in the United States. Not even free African Americans could become citizens, and they were afforded no constitutional protection. Therefore, if law and ethics were the same, in those days if you attempted to subvert the law to give constitutional rights to African Americans, you would not only be violating the law, you would be unethical.

His second example concerned Germany's Nuremberg and other laws, which denied German Jews the rights of German citizenship, and restricted them in many ways. As a German citizen, if you attempted to circumvent these laws or violate them directly, say, by marrying a Jew, officiating at such a marriage, assisting a Jew in the practice of his profession, or failing to report any violation of the laws to the authorities, you would be sent to prison or worse because you violated the law. Were these violators of the law unethical? We can expect punishment if we fail to obey a law whether it is a good law or a bad one, but that has nothing to do with ethics.

Drucker's Early Struggles with Unethical Leadership

In fact, an ethical issue caused Drucker to struggle with the whole concept of leadership. Fleeing Germany at the ascent of Hitler, he was well aware of the excesses and brutality of the Nazis in both Germany and Drucker's native Austria. Hitler, who had taken the very title of *Fuehrer*, or "Leader," clearly did not demonstrate ethical behavior and could not be called a man of integrity or honor. Drucker found other dictators—Mussolini, Stalin, and Mao—equally wanting in this regard. As a result, Drucker's initial approach was to largely ignore the importance of leadership and to assume that it was a concept so basic that there was nothing in it that had not been known since ancient times, and that, in any case, "leadership could not be taught or learned."

At the same time, Drucker analyzed and rejected a commonly held view of business ethics: that the ordinary rules of ethics do not apply to business. Drucker took a decidedly contrary view. He wrote that personal values of right and wrong should *not* be separated from values put into practice at work.[3] However, he took an entirely different tack from what most experts say about business ethics.

Drucker's Analysis of Business Ethics for the Leader

Drucker looked at ethics from various viewpoints. He began with ethical thinking from the Western tradition, beginning with the Bible and up through modern times. I examine many of these viewpoints in the pages ahead. All of these various approaches to ethics do agree on one point: whatever the definition of ethics and proper individual behavior that one embraces, it must apply to everyone alike. However, this tradition did include the concept of extenuating circumstances, whereby clemency might be granted to a violator under certain conditions. "Thou shalt not steal" is one of the Ten Commandments. Yet a mother stealing to feed a starving child might be excused. Differences due to different social or cultural mores might also be mitigating factors. That is, practices of questionable morality in one setting might not only be considered acceptable in another, they could also be considered ethical.[4]

Drucker told a story in class supporting this view, which I have told when teaching ethics and in several of my books:

A large Japanese corporation decided to open an American manufacturing plant. This would bring many jobs to the selected area and many states and cities vied for the opportunity. After investigating various locations, and considering a number of proposals, a site was chosen and after negotiation with local and state officials, the announcement was made. So significant was this event, the president of the Japanese corporation flew in from Japan for the groundbreaking. The local government scheduled an elaborate ceremony with attendant publicity. They invited the state's governor and many other senior state officials as well as company officers and other dignitaries.

The Japanese president spoke English; however, to ensure that everything he said would be understood, the company hired a Nisei, or second-generation American of Japanese descent, to act as translator. This woman held an advanced business degree and was fluent enough in both Japanese and English to translate into English as he spoke. With dignity and in measured tones, the Japanese president began to speak, noting the great honor it was for his company to locate to this part of the United States. After he spoke a couple paragraphs, the interpreter translated his remarks into English.

The Japanese executive noted the mutual benefits to his company, to the area's citizens, to the local economy, and to Japanese-American friendship. Then, nodding in the direction of the governor and other state and local officials present, he said, "Furthermore, Mr. Governor and high officials, our company knows its ethical duty. When the time comes that you retire from your honored positions, my corporation will not forget what you have done and will repay you for the efforts which you have expended in our behalf in giving us this opportunity."

The interpreter was horrified. She instantly decided to omit these remarks from her English translation. The CEO, who understood enough English to realize what she had done, but not why, continued his speech as if nothing had happened. Later, when the two were alone, the CEO asked his interpreter, "How could you exclude my reassurances to the governor and other officials regarding our ethical duty? Why did you leave this important statement out of my speech?" Only then could she explain to his amazement that what is ethical, even a duty, in Japan is considered unethical and even corruption in the United States. The Japanese CEO agreed that the interpreter had acted correctly and told her that in deference to the American view of ethics, he would forgo Japanese custom, and American laws would be obeyed.

Drucker explained further why the actions of the Japanese CEO were considered an ethical duty and neither unethical nor unlawful in Japan. "In Japan," Drucker told us, "government officials are paid very little. They could live on what they receive in retirement only with great difficulty. It is therefore expected that when they retire, companies that have benefited from their actions during their tenure will assist them, financially and otherwise. Since they could barely get by on their retirement, this is considered the only right and ethical thing to do." Drucker concluded that the Japanese CEO acted correctly, because such actions were unethical as well as illegal in the United States.

Drucker on Extortion or Bribery

Drucker noted that bribery was hardly desirable from the viewpoint of the victim from whom a bribe was extorted. A law prohibiting the payment of bribes to obtain foreign contracts had recently been passed in the United States when senior Lockheed Aircraft executives paid bribes to members of the Japanese government who demanded it in exchange for subsidizing the purchase of the L-1011 passenger jet for All Nippon Airways. As a result, Lockheed's chairman and its vice chairman and president were both forced to resign their posts in disgrace early in 1976.[5] They gained nothing personally from the sales of the L-1011.

Why did these two Lockheed executives commit such a stupid act? In the years 1972–73, 25,000 Lockheed employees faced a significant threat of unemployment after cutbacks in the U.S. government order of military aircraft and missiles. Because of delays in delivery of the L-1011's engines, All Nippon Airways was the only major airline that had not committed to purchase a wide-body jet from a competitor. If a major contract could not be secured for the L-1011, many jobs would have been lost.

The two executives gained not a cent in monetary or any other advantage from their act, which they claimed was committed solely to help workers and in the interests of social responsibility. Had Lockheed simply abandoned the L-1011 and not paid the bribe, stock price analysts determined that company earnings, stock price, and bonuses and stock options for the two Lockheed executives involved would have substantially increased. Everyone knew that because of the delays the L-1011 was a loser and could no longer make money. In fact, the project never made any money despite these and other sales. Still, their actions were cited as a gross violation of "business ethics."[6]

Drucker's view was very clear. He thought it stupid to pay bribes. He thought good management required that the L-1011 project should simply have been abandoned.

Were the executives' actions a violation of the law or of business ethics? Most countries have laws against bribery. Yet it is a fact that bribery, as we define it, may be routine and expected in some of these same countries. In Japan, a Japanese CEO's promise to reward government officials who helped his company while the officials were still in office would be seen as a form of bribery, whereas a payment to these same government officials after they were out of office would not. Everyone in Japan understands the difference. In other countries, *baksheesh* (the exchange of money for favors) is the traditional way of doing business, and businesspeople in these countries ignore any laws that may have been enacted against the tradition, seeing them as "window dressing" designed to appease countries with which they trade that do not accept this practice.

Drucker noted that a private citizen who was extorted to pay a bribe to a criminal might be considered stupid or a helpless victim of intimidation. Certainly paying extortion is never desirable. However, this is clearly not an ethical issue for the individual who is forced to pay a bribe.

Drucker strongly objected to the "new business ethics" which asserted that acts that are not immoral or illegal if done by private citizens automatically became immoral or illegal if done by a business organization with no regard for the circumstances. They might be stupid, they might be illegal, and they might be the wrong thing to do. However, they were not necessarily a violation of "business ethics."

The Ethics of Social Responsibility

Drucker next turned to casuistry. This might be called cost-benefit ethics, or ethics for the greater good. Drucker called this "the ethics of social responsibility." Essentially, it says that someone in power, a CEO, a king, a president, has a higher duty if it can be argued that their behavior confers benefits on others. For example, it is wrong to lie, but in the interests of "the country" or "the company," or "the organization," it might be argued that it sometimes has to be done.

From a casuist's view, the bribe paid to the Japanese officials by Lockheed executives was a duty, a higher responsibility since Lockheed's leaders were trying to take care of Lockheed employees, not to benefit themselves. This sounds very high-minded, but Drucker maintained that it was too dangerous a concept to be adopted as business ethics because a business leader might use it to justify what would be clearly be unethical behavior for anyone else.[7] Drucker looked further.

The Ethics of Prudence

To be prudent means to be careful or cautious. It is a rather unusual philosophy for an ethical approach, but it has some benefits.

When I first became an Air Force general, I was sent to a special course for new generals during which we received lectures and advice from senior military and civilian leaders. I do not recall whether the following was said by the secretary of defense or by a senior general, but it struck us as pretty good advice: "Never do anything you wouldn't want seen on the front page of *The Air Force Times*."

Drucker used a similar example. He said that Harry Truman, at the time a U.S. Senator, advised an Army witness before his committee in the early years of World War II: "Generals should never do anything that needs to be explained to a Senate Committee— there is nothing one can explain to a Senate Committee."[8]

This may be good advice for staying out of trouble, but it is not much of a basis for ethical decision making. For one thing, it doesn't tell you anything about the right kind of behavior. For another, there are decisions that a leader must take that are risky and that may be difficult to explain, especially if things go wrong. Nevertheless, they may be the correct decisions to take.

The Ethics of Profit

Drucker also thought through what he called "the ethics of profit." Now this is not what you might think, so don't skip this. Drucker did not say anything about limiting profits. On the contrary, Drucker wrote that it would be socially irresponsible and most certainly unethical if a business did not show a profit at least equal to the cost of capital because failing to do so would waste society's resources.[9]

Drucker believed that the only logical justification for "profit" was that it was a cost. Profit as an ethical "metric" rested on very weak moral grounds as an incentive, which could only be justified if it was a genuine cost, especially if it were the only way to maintain jobs and to grow new ones.[10]

Drucker exhorted business leaders, "Check to see if you are earning enough profit to cover the cost of capital and provide for innovation. If not, what are you going to do about it?"[11]

During the rise in gas prices (prior to their dramatic fall) in 2008, I found the following response by one refining company CEO interesting: when challenged by a congressional investigating committee, he said, "There is no 'profit.' Every dollar goes into exploration or research and development and is needed to run this business." Drucker would have agreed, although this would have probably been extremely difficult for someone not in the oil business to understand or accept, and clearly did not satisfy the committee, confirming Truman's advice to his generals.

Confucian Ethics

Drucker called Confucian ethics "the most successful and most durable of them all." In Confucian ethics the rules are the same for all, but there are some general rules that vary according to five basic relationships, all based on interdependence. These five are superior and subordinate, father and child, husband and wife, oldest brother and sibling, and friend and friend. The right behavior in each case differs in order to optimize the benefits to both parties in each relationship.

Confucian ethics demands equality of obligations, of parents to children and vice versa, of bosses to subordinates and vice versa. All have mutual obligations. Drucker points out that this is not compatible with what is considered business ethics in many countries including the United States, where one side has obligations and the other side rights or entitlements. Though he clearly admires Confucian ethics, which he calls "the ethics of interdependence," they cannot be applied as business ethics, because this system deals with issues between individuals, not groups. According to Confucian ethics, only the law can handle the rights and disagreements of groups.[12]

Drucker's Conclusions About Business Ethics

What about doing things in business that are "clearly unethical"? How did Drucker define business ethics? Can business ethics be defined in this manner? This came up in class, and his response is identical to one that appears in one of his books: "Hiring call girls to entertain visiting executives does not make you unethical. It merely makes you a pimp."[13]

Drucker concluded that business ethics as we know it today is not ethics at all. If ever business ethics were to be codified, Drucker thought it ought to be based on Confucian ethics, focusing on the right behavior rather than misbehavior or wrongdoing. In the meantime, Drucker believed that leaders should adopt the following into their personal philosophy of ethics:

1. The ethics of personal responsibility from the physician Hippocrates: "*Primum non nocere*," which translates as "above all [or first] do no harm."[14]

2. The mirror test: What kind of person do I want to see when I look into the mirror every morning?[15]

Drucker on Ethics for Leaders

- There are many different approaches to ethics; none is 100 percent compatible with what we, in the United States today, consider business ethics.

- Confucian ethics, that is, the ethics of interdependence, probably comes closest to the ideal for what might be called organizational ethics, but is not compatible with current laws and thinking.

- While every leader needs to "do what's right," since this cannot be defined exactly, above all do no harm—and work on passing the mirror test.

CHAPTER 7

Effective Leadership and Personal Integrity

A s we've seen, Drucker made a clear distinction between the law and personal integrity. Personal integrity, he felt, had to be a part of everything that a leader did; without it, leaders had no legitimacy and their followers would eventually desert them. As he wrote, "In military training, the first rule is to instill soldiers with trust in their officers, because without trust they won't fight."[1]

Integrity in Action

The need for personal integrity is integral to all of Drucker's views of leadership. Integrity means adherence to a moral code; particularly, adherence to such a code under all conditions and regardless of whether anyone knows it. To Drucker integrity is critical because "the spirit of an organization is created by the people at the top."[2] The proof that leaders mean what they say is uncompromising integrity of character, which permeates through the organization.[3]

When No One Knows

Major General Perry M. Smith, a retired Air Force general, tells a story about Babe Zaharias, a champion sportswoman in the 1932 Olympics. Later, as a professional golfer, she penalized herself two strokes for accidentally playing the wrong ball after the round she was playing ended. The penalty cost her first place in a major tournament. Later a friend asked her why she'd done it. "After all, Babe," said the friend, "no one saw you. No one would have known the difference." "I would have known," she replied.[4]

Smith himself became involved in a personal integrity issue only a few years after publishing this story.

Putting Yourself at Risk

After leaving the Air Force, Perry Smith became CNN's military analyst. On June 7, 1998, CNN aired a sensational report that U.S. Special Forces, supposedly supported by U.S. Air Commandos, had used a lethal gas called sarin to exterminate U.S. defectors hiding in Laos in 1970. The whole story was blatantly untrue. As *Fortune* magazine said later, "It was quickly obvious that the broadcast about Operation Tailwind and a *Time* magazine story that followed rested on twisted facts and questionable testimony."[5] However, the falseness of this story only became evident after Smith got involved—at considerable risk to his broadcasting career and income.

Smith, who was in the war zone and well acquainted with the Air Commando unit and its operations at the time the incident was supposed to have occurred, went to Thomas Johnson, the president of CNN, and asked him to delay broadcasting so Smith could get the facts together to disprove the allegations. Johnson refused. Smith immediately gave up his high-paying job and resigned from CNN.

CNN lawyers told Smith that if he went public with his allegations, CNN would sue him. Smith disregarded this threat, gathered the facts, and obtained records that proved that the gas used in the Tailwind Operation in Laos was tear gas, not the deadly nerve gas claimed by CNN. He released this information with as much publicity as possible, despite the threats made by CNN lawyers.

The resulting public outcry was so great that CNN and *Time* magazine had to reinvestigate. Floyd Abrams, the independent attorney CNN hired to conduct an investigation, found no evidence to support the charges these organizations had made and recommended that they immediately retract their statements and apologize. Both news organizations offered a public apology. Within weeks, two producers of the broadcast were fired and a third resigned.[6] Eventually all associated with the program were forced out or left CNN.[7] General Smith went on to work as an analyst for CBS and other networks.

Smith's actions ended well. However, he took a great risk, and right does not always win out and nor is the person of integrity always rewarded.

The Mirror Test

One of Drucker's examples did not have such a happy ending. In his example, a high German official assigned to the embassy in London was well on the way to becoming a foreign minister or even Chancellor in 1906 when he declined an assignment he perceived as impacting on his personal integrity. He resigned and it ended his political career. Why did he do it? He could not look at himself in the mirror.[8]

I have seen as many individuals of integrity punished, or at least receiving negative treatment, as rewarded. It can go either way. I know this for a fact, since I went through this type of experience early in my own career, and I was fully prepared for and expected the worst.

My Own Experience of Integrity in Action

I first wrote about this incident after I left the Air Force. Being reluctant to reveal myself as the hero, I used the nom de guerre "Herb," which was a mistake, because I forgot that I had done so, and in answer to a question during a speech, I told the story in the first person. After my presentation, someone in the audience asked me, privately, if I was Herb. He said that at first he was disgusted. He had read my book, and it seemed I had "stolen" Herb's story. From then on, I quit using the disguise. I was Herb—and here is "Herb's" story as I first told it.

> Herb, a young Air Force lieutenant in 1960, was a new navigator on a B-52 aircrew. Among his responsibilities was programming and launching two air-to-ground "cruise" missiles. The missiles were new and still had many problems that hadn't yet been solved. The aircrews in Herb's squadron that had tested them got mixed results. Sometimes the missiles hit right on target. More often, they weren't even close.
>
> Actually, the aircrew really didn't launch the missiles, as each missile cost millions of dollars. The navigator programmed the missiles en route to the launch point, as he would do on an actual launch. This took several hours as Herb updated the missile repeatedly and told its computers where it was, based on data he gathered from other navigational systems. About thirty minutes from the target, Herb put the missile into "simulated launch" mode. He instructed the pilots to follow a special needle indicator on their consoles. If the needle turned right, the pilots turned the aircraft right. If the needle turned left, they turned the aircraft left. When they did this, the aircraft followed the course to the target according to information in the missile's computer and inertial guidance system, thereby following the same course the missiles would fly had they been launched.
>
> Fifteen seconds from the target Herb turned on a tone signal which was broadcast over the radio. On the

ground, a Ground Control Intercept or GCI site tracked Herb's aircraft on radar. At the point where the missile would normally dive into its target, the missile automatically terminated Herb's tone signal. The course the missile would take to the ground once it started its final dive was based on predetermined factors, including the missile's ballistics. Plotting the aircraft's radar track and knowing the missile's ballistics when the tone signal stopped, it was easy for the GCI site to calculate where the missile would impact if it had actually been launched. The missile's accuracy was supposed to depend primarily on the accuracy of the information that Herb gave the missile's computers during the two hours of updating and programming. These practice runs had a major effect on the crews' careers. Crews that got good scores were promoted. Those that did not, were held back. It went that way all the way up the chain of command. Woe to a unit commander when one of his crews got a "bad bomb," or, now, a "bad missile," that is, one that was too far off target from its intended point of impact.

Herb's crewmates were all far more experienced than he was. Herb was a lieutenant, a junior officer, fresh out of flying school. Herb had never been in combat and had never even served on an aircrew. Everyone else on the rest of the crew had thousands of hours of flying time, including combat experience in World War II and Korea. Both the aircraft commander and the senior navigator, who was the bombardier, were senior officers, lieutenant colonels. Herb and his crew had previously flown with missiles. Sometimes they had been okay, but mostly not. All aircrews were having the same experience. However, there were no penalties because all units were given six months to learn to work with the missiles. What no one knew at the time was that the extreme

sensitivity of the missiles and the more complex techniques required to maintain and service them—and not
the aircrews—were causing the problems.

However, the six-month learning period was up. While
on seven-day alert, Herb's aircraft commander called
the crew together. "On our first training mission after
alert, we have missiles that will be graded for the first
time," he said. "We're not going to debate this. We're
going to cheat to make sure we get good scores. All I
want to know from the navigators is how we're going
to do this."

Herb was shocked. As a West Pointer, he had been
taught that you do not lie, cheat, or steal, or tolerate
anyone who does. He had watched classmates who had
a brief lapse and made a false statement, later regret it
and turn themselves in. In those days, there was only
one punishment for an honor violation: separation from
the Academy, which meant they terminated their own
careers upholding the ideal of honor and integrity. This
was expected. Honor was considered more important
than success, and it could not be compromised under
any circumstance.

"That's easy," the senior navigator (who was also the
bombardier) told the aircraft commander. "Don't follow
the missile needle. I'll adjust for the ballistics, and I'll
'bomb' the target using my radar bombsight. All you
have to do is follow the bombsight's needle as we normally do. The tone is the same for the bombsight or the
missile. The GCI site will not know that we're actually
bombing the target. It will be simple, and no one will
know."

Shortly afterwards, Herb's crew was released from their duties after a week on alert with their aircraft loaded with real nuclear weapons against a potential sneak attack by the Soviets. They had three days of crew rest before getting together to plan the mission which would involve the twelve-hour flight with the missiles. The mission would include the simulated missile launch, some regular bomb runs, some navigation and bomb runs at low level, an aerial refueling, and a celestial navigation leg.

The three days were absolute hell for Herb. He was new to the crew and the squadron, but he had heard rumors that this type of cheating was not unusual. Now he was being ordered to do it with the very missiles with which he was entrusted and for which he was responsible. He talked it over with several friends, other young but more experienced officers. They told him not to rock the boat. They told Herb that this sort of thing was routine and that everybody cheated occasionally. If he didn't cheat, they said, it would be the end of his career.

Herb had worked long and hard to enter West Point, and with difficulty managed to make it through his four years there.

Herb had spent a year in navigation school, six months in bombardier school, attended Air Force survival training, and more weeks of B-52 ground and air training. It had totaled six years, not counting three years in the Reserve Officers Training Corps (ROTC) before attending West Point. How could Herb let it all slip away for this one little lie that apparently nobody cared about anyway?

"I was taught 'integrity first,'" said Herb, "that this was the essence of being an officer. Lying is contrary to everything I was taught and believe in."

When Herb's crew met to plan the mission, he asked to speak to his aircraft commander privately. As soon as they were alone Herb told him: "If you want to cheat, that's up to you. But get yourself a new navigator, because I'm not going to do it." Herb's commander was furious and berated him for quite a long time. Then he slammed the door and left. Herb was plenty scared, and thought it was the end of his career.

I want to make an editorial comment: This last paragraph is actually understated. My tough, combat-experienced lieutenant colonel couldn't believe that this wet-behind-the-ears lieutenant was refusing to obey a direct order, even though an order to cheat was hardly a legal order. The verbal abuse I received was extensive, and I literally shook in my boots, thinking my hard-worked-for career was at an end. I had been raised in the Air Force, my father had been an Air Force officer, I knew nothing about anything else, and I had no idea what I was going to do to earn a living to support my family. The airlines had long since stopped using navigators, so even this wasn't an option.

An hour or so later, Herb's commander was still angry when he said he wanted to see Herb alone. Once alone, he said, "Okay. We'll do it your way. But those missiles better be reliable." "I'll do everything possible to make them so, but I won't cheat," answered Herb.

Herb heard later that this commander told someone, "I don't know whether Herb's a good navigator or not, but I trust him. He's honest and he's got guts."

The missiles were reliable. To this day, Herb still doesn't know if he was skilled, lucky, or whether the two very experienced lieutenant colonels had figured out a way to fool their inexperienced young navigator and cheat anyway. Something Herb did know was how far he would go for what he believed to be right, which was all the way. Herb, who later became a general, said: "I believe that knowledge has helped me immensely over the years and I believe that I owe whatever success I have achieved in part to it. In fact, it still affects my thinking today. Had it ended my career then and there, it still would have been worth it for this priceless piece of knowledge about myself."

Over the years, I have seen and worked with many leaders. Some have demonstrated great integrity and gone on to great things. Others have demonstrated great integrity and it cost them their jobs. And yes, I have seen some with no integrity at all be promoted. But, as Drucker said, although followers will forgive a leader much, they will never forgive a lack of integrity. As Shakespeare wrote, "This above all: to thine own self be true, And it must follow, as the night the day, Thou canst not then be false to any man."

Drucker on the Need for Personal Integrity

- Followers will forgive a leader many mistakes, but not a lack of integrity.

- Maintaining your integrity may cost you, but it is worth it.

- Be true to yourself, your values, and your beliefs.

CHAPTER 8

The Seven Deadly Sins of Leadership

S ome say that Drucker turned away from writing for business leaders in the last ten or so years of his life because he saw too many of them display the vices he warned about in his teachings. I cannot speak to this. He said nothing to me about it, and I have found no hard evidence for such a change. Drucker did become more interested in nonprofit leadership during that period. However, Drucker maintained his contact with business leaders of all types and continually wrote about both nonprofit and for-profit management and lectured about them in the classroom.

It is a fact that Drucker set very high ethical standards for all leaders. To Peter, management, as a profession practiced by leaders, was a "calling" regardless of the environment in which it was practiced. He saw leaders as special people entrusted with special organizational as well as societal responsibilities. He knew that leaders were human and sometimes erred, and he was well aware that there were leaders, both in and out of corporations, who did not live up to the high standards he regarded not only as necessary but as part of the code they accepted when they made the decision to accept the mantle of the leader. This was true whether they led a corporation, a church, or a military unit.

In this regard, he thought some leaders failed their profession, the organizations and individuals they led, and society. Some lost sight of the real goals expected of them and the reason they were in their positions of responsibility. Others didn't understand the implications of the responsibilities they had accepted, and put their own interests above those they led. Others were seduced by the power and the privileges that leadership brings. All these shortcomings pained him, and he frequently wrote about them. He hoped that by making these traps explicit he could help leaders avoid falling into them.

Why the Seven Deadly Sins?

To categorize these potential failings, I sought a number of different models including abuse of special privileges, abuse of power, and corruption. None seems to fit all of the cautionary tales Drucker used to warn leaders of all stripes.

Finally, the idea of the seven deadly sins occurred to me while I was asleep. Clearly, this was my subconscious at work. When I compared the seven deadly sins with Drucker's view of where executives go awry, I discovered that they were identical to the traps Drucker cautioned leaders to avoid. In further analyzing the seven deadly sins, I saw that to a great extent avoiding these sins might have saved otherwise outstanding leaders.

The Leadership Sin of Pride

The sin of pride is usually considered the most serious of the seven deadly sins. Yet it seems so innocuous. My wife calls it "being full of yourself." I mean after all, why shouldn't leaders feel proud of their accomplishments? I believe feeling proud of what one has accomplished or is accomplishing is perfectly acceptable. The problem comes when leaders believe themselves so special that ordinary rules no longer apply. Generalized pride—as opposed to being proud of specific things—is the most serious leadership sin because it can easily lead to the other six. Sometimes even the perception of what the leader does while committing this sin will make things far worse.

On May 18, 1993, Bill Clinton stopped in Los Angeles. After his stay, Air Force One was on the runway getting ready to take off from Los Angeles International Airport when Clinton decided to avail himself of the services of an upscale Beverly Hills hair stylist, Cristophe, who had cut Clinton's hair in the past. Cristophe rushed to the airport, boarded Air Force One, and gave Clinton a $200 haircut, upscale for the early 1990s. Reporters aboard Air Force One soon learned the reason for the take-off delay.

The next day it was all over the news, television, radio, newspapers, and the networks: while airliners circled overhead burning fuel impatiently awaiting clearance to land and while other airliners lined up on the ground behind Air Force One, unable to take off, President Clinton got a well-known Beverly Hills hair stylist to cut his hair. Americans were irate. Clinton appeared to be an arrogant and insensitive leader, not at all the individual those who voted for him thought he was. Clinton of course apologized, saying that he did not know the trouble this caused, but it took some time for him to live this incident down, and it harmed his image.

The only problem with this story is that much of it was untrue. Clinton did get a haircut, which took a few minutes, but according to FAA records, the haircut caused no significant delays of regular scheduled flights. There were no circling airplanes and no traffic jams. Still, if for no other reason than the perception of an unwarranted special privilege, he should not have done it. It was a minor incident in the scheme of things—but, unfortunately, it was a harbinger of much more serious things to come that damaged an otherwise highly successful administration.

The Leadership Sin of Lust

I once heard a retired leader of an organization of almost a million members speak about the challenges of leading this organization. "One of the biggest problems," he said, "was a newly promoted senior executive. I may be exaggerating a little," he continued, "but it seems that almost as soon as we promoted him, he suddenly decided that he was God's gift to women."

This individual spoke at a time when almost all senior executives were male. However, I do not think that one would find much difference with female executives. There is unfortunately a feeling among some leaders that they have "arrived" and are "entitled"; sex is seen as some sort of fringe leadership benefit. In one online survey by the *White Stone Journal*, lust was the most frequent of the seven deadly sins self-reported as "my biggest failing."[1] This sin is hardly uncommon. However, it can have very unfortunate consequences. In any workplace, it creates jealousies, feelings of favoritism, and lack of trust, damaging people and relationships and more.

While organizations often prefer to conceal sexual scandals and force the leader quietly out of office, many times this is not possible with political and public institutions, which are closely watched by media quick to publish even suspicions of misconduct. So we frequently know the consequences of the leader's actions. Hardly a month goes by without the media reporting a leader for this vice. The problems created for leaders because of this deadly sin seem almost without limit.

Clearly, sex is a major psychological drive. Napoleon Hill, author of perhaps the greatest motivational book in modern times, *Think and Grow Rich*, suggested that by rechanneling sexual energy into other areas, considerable success might be achieved. Rechanneling sexual involvement in the workplace probably is the best idea.

Drucker didn't seem to care much about these activities in and of themselves. He seemed to believe that a leader's individual morals were up to that individual, except where it affected the organization and the leader's performance as a leader. However, Drucker thought that leaders did not pay enough attention to avoiding this particular deadly leadership sin, and thought that leaders could do a better job of avoiding problems that affected their ability to lead.

The Leadership Sin of Greed

The sin of greed is a sin of excess. It frequently starts with power. Leaders have power, and unfortunately having power has a tendency to lead to corruption if the leader isn't careful. This may start with the acceptance of small favors and grow into accumulating vacations, bribes, and worse.

Randy "Duke" Cunningham was a real naval hero during the Vietnam War. Wounded in action, he received a Navy Cross, the highest award next to the Congressional Medal of Honor, for bravery in battle. He was one of a handful of ace fighter pilots who shot down five or more enemy aircraft in that war. He served the Navy for twenty-one years; later, he was elected to Congress, where he served for almost fifteen years. However, on November 28, 2005, Cunningham pled guilty to a variety of charges and resigned his seat in Congress. He admitted to taking $2.4 million dollars in bribes from defense contractors, and was sentenced to eight years and four months in prison. This was the longest sentence ever given a former congressman in a corruption case. On receiving sentence, he said, "I misled my family, staff, friends, colleagues, the public—even myself. For all of this, I am deeply sorry. The truth is—I broke the law, concealed my conduct, and disgraced my high office."[2]

How do these things happen? Usually a leader sees others with more possessions, more power, more privilege. Like Cunningham, such a leader probably has quite a few accomplishments on record. The leader may wonder why others have so much more, when (in the leader's mind) they are far less deserving. This sin is closely associated with the sin of envy.

Maybe a small bribe is accepted. The leader may not even see it as a bribe, just a favor between friends. If the leader allows seduction to take place, greed can take over, resulting in a tearful confession like Congressman Cunningham's. Despite the claim in the movie, greed was never "good," even as a motivator, and though Drucker analyzed and approved many motivators, greed was not one of them.

I should not leave this discussion of the sin of greed without noting the terrible contribution greed made to the economic meltdown that began in late 2008. Call it gluttony (which I will discuss shortly) or greed, it is not something the ethical leader participates in.

The Leadership Sin of Sloth

For the leader, the sin of sloth is associated with an unwillingness to act. Sometimes this is laziness. More often, it is an unwillingness to do work the leader considers beneath the dignity of the office. I have many times seen leaders watching critical work they could do as well as anyone—standing around "supervising" when they could have given real help to their subordinates and to the mission for which they were responsible.

Aaron Bloom was brought in to take over a company that two years earlier he had served as vice president. The former president was gone, the company was a shadow of its former self with only 50 employees (it formerly had 350), and was now under Chapter 11 bankruptcy protection. The company was short of money and resources of all kinds.

Bloom insisted that all company officers, including himself, work on the production line under the supervision of line supervisors after hours to fulfill an important order and get a needed inflow of cash started. He didn't stand around watching. He worked the production line like an hourly employee. He did not practice the sin of sloth. As president, he returned the company to its former status and worked it out of Chapter 11 in two years. He went on to lead it until he retired, fifteen years later.

As his army moved toward a critical battle, the Emperor Napoleon and his staff and several senior Marshals of France, all mounted on horses, came upon an artillery caisson mired in the mud and blocking the passage of his troops. A dozen soldiers were struggling to free it. Napoleon immediately jumped from his horse, and put his own shoulder to the effort, saying "Boys, we'll get it free together." Naturally, his staff and the be-medaled Marshals of France present soon joined him. They freed the cannon, remounted, and went on their way, and Napoleon's army eventually won the battle. Is it any wonder why Napoleon's troops followed him in the most difficult conditions again and again?

During World War II, Air Force Major General Hoyt Vandenberg commanded the 9th Tactical Air Force in Europe. He happened to be visiting an airbase when a gunner, suffering from combat fatigue after flying repeated missions with high losses, suddenly "cracked" and shouted that he couldn't fly that day. Rather than rebuke the young gunner, Vandenberg said, "That's okay, son. You don't need to fly today. I'm qualified as an aerial gunner, and I'll fly for you." He did. It saved a good gunner, who returned to flight status and was able to complete his tour of duty honorably and successfully. Vandenberg went on to become chief of staff of the Air Force.

In the last article that Peter Drucker wrote for the *Wall Street Journal* before his death, he stated that American CEOs were unique and that the concept of the CEO as conceived in the United States, and with the responsibilities of the CEO, did not exist in any other country. These responsibilities, Drucker said, not only included work that only the CEO could do but also the requirement to do it.[3] In Drucker's view, these responsibilities involved dealing with things outside the organization and deciding what to do about them. Unfortunately, some CEOs abdicated these and many other responsibilities, which fall under the heading of the sin of sloth.

Failing to know what is going on in your organization is also an abdication of responsibility. Kenneth Lay, Enron CEO, proclaimed his innocence in the fall of Enron right up until his death. However, even if Lay knew nothing of the illegal machinations that led to Enron's collapse, and one of Enron's vice presidents did testify in support of this statement, he was still guilty of abdicating his responsibilities in a way that led to the demise of his company. Leaders are responsible for everything that their organization does or fails to do, and nothing can absolve a leader of this responsibility.

Leaders do not sit around when they are needed. They don't ignore their responsibilities. Both are examples of the sin of sloth and lead to disaster. Leaders are proactive and they take action.

The Leadership Sin of Wrath

This sin has to do with uncontrolled anger. There is a time for anger in leadership when it serves a definite and useful purpose. As Kenneth Blanchard and Spencer Johnson taught us in *The One Minute Manager*, you can take one minute to make a correction, include the words "I'm angry," and then tell the recipient why.[4] Moreover, anger does have a useful function in that it can mobilize psychological and physical resources to do something about a problem.

However, leaders need to avoid repeated and uncontrolled anger because it can damage their leadership. It can destroy morale. It does not guarantee a lasting effect in correcting problems, and its constant application makes it useless as a tool at the times when expressing it would really be helpful and appropriate.

Moreover, when in an angry state, the leader loses the capacity to self-monitor and the ability to observe objectively.

If nothing else, Drucker taught leaders to analyze their environment and to determine what actions that had already occurred meant for the future before taking action. Using anger as a single response to all leadership challenges precludes doing this analysis. It prevents the leader from making good decisions and perhaps from taking the action appropriate to the situation. Actions taken during uncontrolled anger are almost invariably in error and require additional work to undo their consequences later.

The Leadership Sin of Envy

With the sin of envy, the leader is envious of what is enjoyed by someone else. This may or may not be accompanied by greed. The sin usually leads the leader to make decisions and to take actions that will harm the object of the envy.

A leader who falls victim to this sin may deny an earned promotion to a qualified subordinate, attempt to destroy another's reputation, or in other ways attempt to feel better by lowering the status of another. This is obviously harmful to the other individual and hurts the organization, and it is probably harmful to the leader who perpetrates these actions.

The Leadership Sin of Gluttony

Most associate food or drink with this sin, but for the leader it has a far more ominous connotation. Of all the deadly sins, gluttony is the one that most frustrated Drucker. Expensive food or drink is scarce; therefore, excessive consumption can be seen as a sign of status, but gluttony does not apply only to food.

Drucker had defended perceived high executive salaries in his early writings. He knew how hard executives had to work and how much they had to do without to reach the pinnacle of their careers.

However, by the time I became his student in the mid-1970s, sky-rocketing executive salaries caused him to alter his opinion drastically. He said that executive salaries at the top had become clearly excessive and that the ratios of the compensation of American top managers to the lowest-paid workers were the highest in the world. The ratio of average U.S. CEO compensation to average pay of a U.S. nonmanagement employee hit a high in 2001 of 525 to 1.[5] He said this was morally wrong and recommended a ratio of no more than 20 to 1.[6]

In class, he debunked the arguments for such enormous pay differentials. In response to the proposition that top executives deserved these salaries because of the performance of the corporations they headed, he noted that many top executives were paid these salaries even when their organizations suffered enormous losses or as they led companies into bankruptcy.

Nor were these salaries needed to attract the most qualified executives. He pointed to examples of several well-known companies that were performing very well but whose chief executives were paid much more modest salaries. One was Avis Rent A Car. Its president, Robert Townsend, was well known for the "We Try Harder" advertising campaign and his relatively modest salary had a significant effect on Avis's success during his tenure. Townsend actually refused to leave the room when his board of directors tried to raise his salary and made it plain that this was a leadership issue, stating, "This would be counterproductive to everything I'm trying to accomplish."

Drucker did not win many friends among high executives with his injunction about too high salaries. Once awarded, an excessive benefit like this is hard to give up. It's easy to rationalize—and a status issue. However, there was no question in Drucker's mind but that executive hypercompensation was an accurate example of the sin of gluttony and was to be avoided for good leadership. Interestingly, he drew a parallel between high executive salaries and the demands of unions for more and more benefits without an increase in productivity. He said we would pay a terrible price for these examples of gluttony and that it is never pleasant to watch hogs gorge. As I write these words, this is exactly what we are witnessing.

Drucker on What a Leader Should Avoid

I have characterized the vices that Drucker counseled leaders to avoid as the Seven Deadly Sins of Leadership:

- The Sin of Pride
- The Sin of Lust
- The Sin of Greed
- The Sin of Sloth
- The Sin of Wrath
- Sin of Envy
- The Sin of Gluttony

There are things that leaders must do, and things they must not. These are the things Drucker maintained that leaders must not do.

CHAPTER 9

Effective Leadership and Corporate Social Responsibility

D rucker recognized and was one of the first to teach that people were not a cost—they were a resource. In his view, workers in and out of the workplace were as much the responsibility of the corporate leader as profits, survival, and growth of the business or organization. Social responsibility and leadership went hand in hand. Therefore, it should come as no surprise that Drucker wrote and taught about the social responsibilities of business and how these responsibilities could best be implemented by corporate leaders. Consequently, Drucker, the "Father of Modern Management," was also called a pioneer of business social responsibility. Drucker believed it was an important part of ethics, which he saw as a necessary condition for effective leadership. However, once again there was a Drucker difference.

The Drucker Difference

Peter Drucker's differences with most of those who thought and wrote about the social responsibility of organizations are found in six main themes:

- Inability of government to solve social problems

- Corporate mission first

- Unlimited liability clause on unintended consequences

- Ethics of social responsibility

- Opportunities for competitive advantage

- Critical importance of leadership

Inability of Government to Solve Social Problems

Drucker became increasingly disenchanted with government's ability to initiate or implement successful social programs. In 1984, he noted, "There is now no developed country—whether free enterprise or communist—in which people still expect government programs to succeed."[1] He pointed to a number of reasons for the increasing failure of government to assume responsibility for social problems or achieve worthwhile results, including a scarcity of first-rate people to implement social programs, impatience and the limited time in which government expected to achieve success, and the inability of government to experiment. However, the overriding reason was that government, by necessity, served too many constituencies with different goals and different values, which made it extremely difficult, if not impossible, to set specific goals and objectives. Frequently what goals and objectives it did recognize were mutually exclusive, and without consistent, agreed-upon goals and objectives, any social program was hopeless from the start.[2] Drucker saw that when seeking to solve social problems, government is frequently confronted with conflicting "theres" that cannot be easily resolved.

Various aspects of the U.S. welfare system provide an important example. Started during the Great Depression of 1929–1941, the idea was to help the poor and enable them to persevere during this time of extreme economic trauma. However, once started, successful or unsuccessful, any government social program is difficult to terminate. Moreover, the initiation of one program provides the motivation for others. This confirmed Drucker's reservations about the limitations and dangers of government management in these areas.

Initially, the most common form of welfare payment was a program called Aid to Families with Dependent Children (AFDC), which was designed to help children whose fathers had died. Over time, AFDC evolved into the main source of income for millions of poor American families; some believe it inadvertently encouraged out-of-wedlock birth, especially among the teenage poor. For instance, by 1995, an unmarried woman with no income could receive, depending on need, as much as $688 per month.[3] One factor determining need was the number of dependent children. So the more children teenage women had, the greater their income. Some believed the government, in attempting to assume social responsibility in this area, was not only failing but encouraging teen pregnancy and the breakdown of the family, discouraging work, and was habituating generations of poor to living on welfare as their sole source of income. The program seemed to be doing little to reduce poverty.[4] In 1996, a new law replaced AFDC with local programs financed by federal grants. The new law limited lifetime welfare assistance to five years and required most adults to work after two years on welfare.[5] It did not solve the problem, but it did lessen its impact.

Corporate Mission First

According to Drucker, the organization's first responsibility is always to its own mission regardless of other factors. If an effort to achieve a positive benefit resulted in harm to the organization initiating it, it was not socially responsible, regardless of good intentions. The first "social responsibility" of business is to make a profit sufficient to cover future operational costs. He reasoned that if the organization failed in its own goals because of misallocation of time, resources, or personnel in order to fulfill some social responsibility, not only would it not solve that or future social problems, it would fail society by not providing products, services, jobs, and its contribution to the economy. Once the organization failed in its primary mission, there was no need for it and it would go out of existence. Thus, if this basic "social responsibility" is not met, no other "social responsibility" can be met either.[6]

This was controversial when Drucker conceived it, and is still controversial. Advocates for various causes frequently pressure organizations to resolve social issues or solve social problems that are totally outside the organization's area of expertise or ability to comply. These demands are made even though the actions desired by these groups, if adopted, might hurt the organization itself, and in some instances might hurt society as well. Failing to take the action desired, these organizations are sometimes termed "greedy" or "unethical" or worse.

Although Drucker recognized the need for nongovernmental organizations to assume responsibility for solving social problems, he added an important caveat: they must above all do nothing to impede their own capacity to perform their obligations to their mission, profitability (including the cost of capital), or need for innovation.

Unlimited Liability Clause on Unintended Consequences

As noted in the preceding section, good intentions are of themselves not necessarily socially responsible, particularly when accepting a particular responsibility might hurt the organization's ability to accomplish its mission. However, more common, and even more serious, is when an organization takes actions aimed at improving a social condition where the result has a significant and unintended negative impact.

An unlimited liability clause means that the organization assumes the responsibility for the outcome of an action, no matter what. It is not just for the present, but also into the future. Most advocates and consumers view high prices as a social ill that must be addressed and reduced. Sam Walton recognized this need and in the process built his company, Wal-Mart, into the world's largest retailer. Of course, Walton didn't charge low prices for reasons of social responsibility. He recognized that consumers wanted low prices and charged them to gain competitive advantage. By focusing on the low prices demanded, Walton transformed retailing. By adopting this as a business strategy, Wal-Mart made a positive social impact. For example, Wal-Mart's decision early in its corporate history to save costs by eliminating paper packaging for personal products helped save millions of trees globally. It changed how manufacturers packaged and sold their products to retailers and it saved labor and waste. Through Wal-Mart's rigid low margin and big quantity purchasing, it forced its suppliers to alter their environmental and cost-saving practices and to focus on low pricing, which benefited the consumer.

Unfortunately for Wal-Mart, its policies had unintended results for which it was eventually held accountable. The same strategies that earlier brought profit, success, and cheers from consumers, eventually brought worldwide legal problems, government interference, and bad press. Although Wal-Mart sought to build in areas where competitors were not located, years later, its presence in cities grew and expanded. Wal-Mart was accused of forcing out smaller local business, which could not compete with Wal-Mart's low prices. In addition, Wal-Mart kept prices down in part by closely controlling and limiting the pay and benefits of its employees. Suppliers who felt obligated to deal with the colossus that Wal-Mart had become accused the company of squeezing them into bankruptcy. Some studies claimed that Wal-Mart's practices had forced jobs into overseas markets to ensure low prices.[7] Wal-Mart had gone from corporate "good guy" to corporate "bad actor" without changing anything.

Drucker taught that since impacts are inevitable, the first thing that an organization needs to do to be socially responsible is to minimize them and not to do foolish things in the name of "doing good." Once again leaders must "look out the window" to observe what is likely to happen as a result of their actions and to note both intended and unintended results. The same kind of fact gathering, analysis, and thoughtful planning needs to be done as with any major investment of time, resources, and personnel for the organization's primary mission.

Potential impacts must be identified and analyzed, and actions whose impacts could damage the organization's primary mission should be dropped, or at least minimized, no matter how socially responsible they appear to be. Of course as time goes on and the environment changes, everything needs to be reexamined.

The Ethics of Social Responsibility

Drucker struggled with the concept of the ethics of social responsibility. He did not find an exact solution that would cover all contingences, although he did feel that several basic Confucian concepts provided general guidelines. One Western guideline— *primum non nocere*—"first, do no harm"—provided guidance in applying the difficult task of ethics to social responsibility.[8] According to Drucker, this injunction should be applied in the area of social responsibility as well as general business ethics.

Opportunities for Competitive Advantage in Social Responsibility

Today social responsibility is the in thing. Many corporations have entire departments to encourage social responsibility, examine company actions that might have negative impacts, uncover opportunities, and develop and run social responsibility programs.

It is easy to forget that this was not always so, and that once even Alfred P. Sloan, legendary CEO of General Motors, claimed that social responsibility was not the responsibility of business and that the two should remain completely and forever separate. In one of the very rare disagreements with Sloan's management precepts, Drucker proclaimed that fulfilling social responsibility was not only a duty but could provide competitive advantages to a company beyond mere public relations.

As Drucker saw it, even a company's negative impacts could and should be examined to turn, if possible, something that the company was doing that was causing harm into something positive. He saw that in the early 1920s DuPont, a major chemical company, set out to eliminate some of the poisonous and unwanted by-products of its manufacturing. In the process, it invented a new system of toxin control that was so successful that it developed it as a separate business. DuPont was not alone. The Dow Chemical Company, another leading U.S. chemical firm, realized the company was causing air and water pollution problems. This was long before environmentalists began to protest the harmful impact that industries were having on the environment. On its own and without coercion, Dow not only adopted a zero pollution policy for its manufacturing facilities, it also focused its considerable research muscle on turning pollutants, including smokestack gasses, into products it was able to sell profitably.[9] Yes, it is the old lemons-into-lemonade idea, but it has been very successful for the companies attempting it.

Julius Rosenwald first became vice president and treasurer, and later president, of an ailing and unprofitable Sears Roebuck and Company. Under his leadership, sales climbed from $750,000 a year to over $50 million. Rosenwald invested a lot of money over the course of his life in social programs, including $70 million for schools, colleges, and universities (among them, the African American Tuskegee Institute—in 1912, a time when prejudice was more in vogue than equal opportunity).[10] Although Rosenwald was a city boy who probably knew nothing about farming, he put a lot of money into agriculture. He implemented the many socially responsible policies because it was the right thing to do, but he also saw that the welfare of the company was primarily based on the knowledge, skill, and well-being of the company's primary customer, which then was the American farmer. Rosenwald's social responsibility had a dual purpose. It not only helped people, it built Sears Roebuck's customer base and developed its market. Within ten years, the company went from near bankruptcy to being the largest merchant in the world and one of America's most profitable and fastest-growing companies. Social responsibility was a major competitive advantage![11]

The issue of workplace diversity has been a major social responsibility concern for many years, not only in a multicultural society like the United States but, because of the growth of multinational corporations and globalization, any organization in any country with dealings outside of its own national boundaries. There are specific advantages to workplace diversity that help make it a major competitive advantage:

- Greater adaptability and flexibility during rapid change

- The ability to attract and retain the most talented employees

- The reduction of costs associated with turnover, absenteeism, and low productivity

- Greater return on investment from various initiatives, policies, and practices

- The ability to gain and keep greater or new market share (locally and globally) with an expanded and diverse customer base

- Increased sales and profits[12]

One example is IBM, whose original approach to eliminating discrimination was to simply ignore cultural, racial, and other differences among its worldwide workforce of more than 150,000 employees. When Lou Gerstner became CEO in 1993, he dropped this concept and initiated a diversity task force with a different approach and a different objective. The new objective was to uncover and understand the differences among the groups making up the IBM workforce and the markets they served, and then to use what it learned to find ways to appeal to a broader set of employees and customers. It worked, and understanding and using its diversity became a major competitive advantage for IBM. Because of Gerstner's initiative, the number of female executives in the company grew 370 percent and the number of ethnic minority executives increased by 233 percent. It led to efforts to develop a broader client base among businesses owned by women, Asians, African Americans, Hispanics, senior citizens, and Native Americans. This in turn resulted in a dramatic growth in revenue in the company's small and medium-sized business sales—from ten million to hundreds of millions of dollars in just five years.[13]

Not only American companies have secured significant competitive advantages through social responsibility initiatives. Toyota introduced the Prius, a hybrid electric/gasoline automobile, after experiments to control harmful emissions. The vehicle it developed reduced emissions to 10 percent of what was formerly acceptable and decreased gasoline consumption by as much as 50 percent. This put Toyota so far ahead of its competitors that other automobile companies licensed Toyota's technology.[14] At Toyota itself, the system is a feature on more than one million vehicles sold. Using social responsibility as a competitive advantage, Toyota surpassed General Motors as the world's largest automaker.

The Critical Importance of Leadership

Drucker knew that nothing effective could be done, including about social responsibility, without good leadership, especially at the top of the organization. Without Rosenwald's leadership, there would have been no example for Sears Roebuck to follow. In this sense, social responsibility and good leadership are interdependent. There cannot be effective leadership without social responsibility, but social responsibility also requires good leadership.

Drucker on Leadership and Social Responsibility

Drucker's concepts regarding social responsibility have stood the test of time. They require leaders to think, and to have the courage and make the effort to take action where appropriate. They are based on the belief that

- Government cannot solve social problems

- Corporate mission comes first

- Unintended negative consequences must considered whenever they occur

- The ethics of social responsibility require "first, do no harm"

- Opportunities for competitive advantage in social responsibility offer substantial benefit

- Leadership is critically important

Those who follow Drucker's ideas will not necessarily have an easy time, but their contribution to their organizations and to society will be of immense benefit.

CHAPTER 10

The Responsibility of a Corporation
First, Do No Harm

D rucker summarized what he expected from the leader with *primum non nocere*; in plain English, "above all, do no harm." Drucker was only partly correct in his description of the origin of this cautionary instruction, but his conclusion is so important that it requires a separate discussion.

Hippocrates was a physician born in 460 B.C. on the Greek island of Kos. As Peter Drucker is known as the "Father of Modern Management," Hippocrates is known as the "Father of Medicine." In the ancient world (at least the known Western civilization), Hippocrates was regarded as the greatest physician of his day. In the same manner that Drucker looked at a business, Hippocrates looked at a patient and based his diagnoses on his observations. This was a breakthrough at the time. Hippocrates rejected the accepted views of his age that attributed illness to evil spirits or the disfavor of the gods. Drucker shared other things in common with Hippocrates. Hippocrates believed that the body must be looked at as a whole and not as individual parts to be analyzed, diagnosed, and treated separately. He observed symptoms and was the first to accurately describe and catalog indications of various illnesses. He developed the Oath of Medical Ethics, now known as the Hippocratic Oath, which is still affirmed by most new physicians as they begin practicing Western medicine. It is said to be one of the oldest binding documents in history. According to the American Medical Association, the Oath "has remained in Western civilization as an expression of ideal conduct for the physician."

The Hippocratic Oath and *Primum Non Nocere*

It is interesting to note that the statement "above all, do no harm," is not in the Hippocratic Oath. About the closest one comes to it are the words. "I will apply dietetic measures for the benefit of the sick according to my ability and judgment; I will keep them from harm and injustice."[1] There is a great deal of controversy about the origins of the phrase, "above all, do no harm," but there is a significant connection to Hippocrates because a close approximation of the phrase can be found in the Hippocratic Corpus: "to help, or at least to do no harm," which comes from Hippocrates' *Epidemics* or *Of the Epidemics*.[2]

Accordingly, we can forgive Drucker this slight inaccuracy since it is the concept *primum non nocere*, and not the text from which it is drawn, that is important. Hippocrates was cautioning the physician to consider the possible harm that any intervention might do the patient. Drucker expands this, in essence cautioning the leader to consider the possible harm that any action taken might cause the mission, the organization, its members, or society. Moreover, he considers this should be the ultimate guide for the leader in ethical conduct in business.

A simple reading of Drucker's advice may give the impression that following it is easy; this is not so. Frequently, well-intentioned acts of leaders can do precisely what Hippocrates and Drucker cautioned against, harm. The harm done can be much greater than the good originally sought. For this reason, leaders must incorporate *primum non nocere* in their overall plan of ethics.

Ensuring No Harm Is Done

There are several ways that leaders can, with the best of intentions, cause harm to the organizations or others and fall into this ethical trap. Most start with the best of intentions: to make some situation better through a positive action. In many cases, the focus of the leader or leaders is so much on the one good intention that the system is not considered as a whole. In other words, the focus is on a part instead of the whole; as a result, "the part" may be better, but the solution may have a negative effect on the whole; that is, the organization, its members, or society.

Moreover, as noted, Drucker taught that good intentions were not in themselves socially responsible. When social responsibilities are undertaken that hurt the organization's ability to accomplish its mission, the resulting harm is the reverse of social responsibility. Even more serious, when organizations ignore this concept and take actions intending to improve a condition, frequently a social condition, they are not absolved from responsibility for whatever unintended negative impacts may ensue.

Pollution from motor vehicles has received a lot of attention over the last thirty years. Despite this, you will see some quiet modification of the strict policies in coming years despite the cry for even more strict control. To eliminate, or reduce, pollution, both states and the U.S. government passed laws limiting auto emissions. The average pollution emitted by an American car manufactured since 2000 is only about 10 percent of that emitted by a car manufactured in the 1960s.[3] Yet we have more pollution from automobiles than ever before. According to the Sierra Club, technological improvements to reduce emissions have mostly been offset by the increase in number of cars on the road, the number of inefficient light trucks and sport utility vehicles, and the number of miles driven each day.

This is partly true. However, this explanation ignores another important factor in the system. The use of pollution-emission reduction devices on automobiles has a negative effect on fuel economy. Therefore, a car driven the same number of miles burns additional fuel per mile to do so. Therefore, for a given number of miles, more fuel must be produced. This, in turn, requires that more oil be refined for this car to drive the same number of miles. Oil refining is a much greater potential source of pollution than automobile operation. Therefore, unless pollution that comes from refining is also reduced, more pollution will result for this car to drive the same number of miles. It's all part of the body or system.

Unintended consequences resulting from good ethical intentions are frequently negative and counterproductive if the results are not thought through using a *primum non nocere* criterion. Various aspects of the U.S. welfare system as it developed are another example of unintended consequences, as described in Chapter Nine.

Look Before Leaping

In the 1990s, the United States was in the midst of the quality revolution, which had some good results—and quite a few bad ones. In the enthusiasm for the new "revolutionary" focus where the emphasis was on the process and not on the outcome, some leaders violated every principle of management and leadership learned over the past seven thousand years and eagerly followed consultants who certainly knew less than they did.

A division of a major corporation surprised several thousand employees when they came to work one morning. Without warning employees were instructed to climb aboard waiting buses, which took them several miles away to a large aircraft hangar.

No one except those behind this action had any idea of what was going on.

On arrival, the employees were disembarked, gathered together, and told that they were fired. However, if they wished (I repeat these words tongue in cheek) they could reapply if they could justify their work position or restructure it such that it was justified to upper management.

On the advice of consultants and human resource personnel, the company shut down for the day while the entire organization went through this rather bizarre exercise. I think the idea was to raise the productivity and the understanding of each member's contribution, to determine where everyone fit, eliminate useless jobs, and maybe unproductive people. However, I was told by participants that it was a madhouse and little other than chaos and insecurity resulted.

The consultants had a preconceived template of how things should be, and the newly designed jobs were structured according to the template. Fortunately, the workers were less gullible and more practical than the company's leaders and managed to work around the crazy quilt organization that resulted after this day of spirited but confusing activity. Eventually things drifted back to normal, although the shutdown, its effect on morale, and working around the Frankenstein monster that the shutdown created probably cost the company a bundle in productivity.

Did the company's CEO intend to create such a mess? Of course not. He was an intelligent leader who wanted to establish his organization in the forefront of the new total quality movement. However, in failing to look closely at what the "experts" were advising, he didn't follow Drucker or Hippocrates and ended up with unintended consequences. He sought to do good, but definitely caused harm. He probably forgot, or didn't know, another of Drucker's insights: Reorganization is always major surgery and attempted only as a last resort.

Never Change for the Good Without First Considering the Future

Any leader, taking any action, assumes the responsibility for the outcome. No leader in any organization is exempt. Drucker's favorite example of this was a Union Carbide plant built with the very best of intentions.

Union Carbide, one of the oldest chemical and polymers companies in the United States, has been a wholly owned subsidiary of the Dow Chemical Company since 2001. The company came out of World War II with a strong reputation for developing raw materials for the chemical and metals industries that helped win the war. Expanding its capabilities and concerned with its social responsibilities, in 1951 Union Carbide decided to locate one of its new plants in a depressed area where unemployment was a major social problem.

After a search for a suitable location that needed Union Carbide's help, the president's staff thought they found exactly the right place, the small town of Vienna in West Virginia. For various reasons, the area was not economically suited for manufacturing. Nevertheless, Union Carbide opened one of its most advanced state-of-the-art plants in a small isolated town and instantly created two thousand to twenty-five hundred new jobs. It even installed the latest anti-pollution equipment, which trapped 75 percent of the ash from its smokestacks, at a time when trapping 50 percent was the best anyone else could achieve. Union Carbide received a lot of good publicity and it was considered a corporate hero when the plant opened. However, its accomplishment was not appreciated for very long. Ten years later, the country had become much more aware of the dangers of pollution. A new mayor was elected on an anti-pollution platform. Everyone knew whom he was attacking. There was only one company in the area, thus the only pollution came from the Union Carbide plant.

Union Carbide, hurt and amazed, fought back. What was the matter with these guys, anyway? Didn't they know that the only reason that Union Carbide came to the area was to do a good deed and to create twenty-five hundred jobs in a totally depressed area? Union Carbide defended itself vigorously, but pollution had become a popular cause and the company soon found itself at war with the state government, the federal government, the environmentalists, and the media.

All this, and the plant was barely economical! Its good intentions were pursued at considerable cost to the company. It certainly never set out to pollute and had even used the very latest anti-pollution equipment when it built the plant. It made little difference. The federal government made threats, and Union Carbide received little support from anyone, including those in the town who had previously benefited. The fight dragged on. Even the usually friendly business media did not support Union Carbide. *Business Week* published an article in February 1971 titled, "A Corporate Polluter Learns the Hard Way."

In frustration and probably some feelings of retaliation Union Carbide announced that the plant would have to be closed as it could not be brought up to environmental standards and remain economically feasible. Union Carbide couldn't win that way either. Union Carbide was heavily criticized for this decision also. Not only was it a polluter, it didn't care about its employees! Public opinion forced Union Carbide to keep the plant open at great cost and no profit.

Drucker concluded that Union Carbide could have avoided many of its problems by simply accepting responsibility when pollution became an important factor, but primarily that the plant should never have been built in the first place. Its location made it certain that any plant built in the area would be uneconomical.[4] The leaders forgot the basic rule of ethics, the one that has no time limit: above all, do no harm.

The Great Housing Depression

As the housing problems of 2007 deepened into crisis in 2008, fingers pointed in all directions. Rooted in the mid-1990s and the goal of making home ownership open to all Americans, key laws were changed and the government, in the name of this good intention, encouraged the mortgage industry to lower lending standards. As a part of this effort, the U.S. Department of Housing and Urban Development formulated policies that fueled the trends toward issuing increasingly risky loans, and directed government-sponsored enterprises that at least 42 percent of the mortgages they purchased should be issued to borrowers whose household income was below the median in their area.

Meanwhile, the economy and housing prices continued to expand. Laws were further loosened, permitting and even encouraging borrowing for homes based not so much on what the prospective homeowners could afford as on how much they could borrow. These practices also encouraged investors to borrow money and, whenever and wherever possible, to purchase multiple properties in order to make money in a market that appeared certain. In nine years, subprime loans rose by 1000 percent.

It was always assumed that a bank cares about whether the loans it makes are repaid, and therefore it would carefully screen potential borrowers. In the 1970s and 1980s, this was in fact the case. The bank that originated a mortgage usually held it for the long term and derived income from interest plus from repayment of the principal. As a result, banks created only those mortgages that were likely to be repaid. However, once the goal of having a greater percentage of Americans become homeowners was attained, various riskier financial innovations—mortgage-backed securities—were developed and permitted that changed this basic principle. For example, mortgages could be broken into component parts so that the principal could be separated from the interest, and the components packaged into securities related only by common characteristics, such as maturity or perceived risk, that could be sold in the financial markets. These caused a number of results that should have been seen as potentially harmful, but were not. High yields in a time of low interest rates were very attractive to Wall Street and these mortgage-backed securities developed quickly into a large market. Nothing wrong with that—except that many banks and specialized mortgage companies no longer held the mortgages they originated. Their main source of revenue was the origination fee, not the repayment of mortgage principal and interest as had been true in the past. As a result, lenders were not concerned about repayment; they were out to make as many of these loans possible under the much more lenient laws that permitted this. The potentially harmful results of these changes should have been foreseen, but were not.

Very good intentions created a toxic mix of incentives, which led to real harm when the bubble burst. If one interjects human greed, which easily clouds judgment when "everybody's doing it," a major disaster was simply waiting to occur. On one side, borrowers were encouraged to borrow and to purchase far more than they could afford. It seemed that they would even make money on these deals as housing prices went higher and higher. The lenders were encouraged to approve as many mortgages as possible since the market was so heated that they would be able to sell the mortgages in these packages before any repayment problems arose, even for clearly risky borrowers. At the same time, increasingly less regulated financial controls made it easy for borrowers, lenders, and financial investment institutions to profit—at least on paper—until everything came crashing down. Above all, do no harm![5]

Drucker on Doing No Harm

- Good intentions don't count for anything.

- Beware of unintended consequences.

- Look before you leap, especially when the concepts are new and the ideas untested.

- Not doing harm counts in the future, too.

PART THREE

The Military: Drucker's Model Organization

One of Drucker's five components of effective leadership had to do with following the recommendations of a classic book on military leadership. Although Drucker left many clues in his writings, I was first led to this conclusion in the classroom by Peter's favorable comparison of the compensation of military to corporate executives. Drucker was very much against excessive compensation. He pointed out that even top executives in the military, responsible for tens of thousands of individuals and millions of dollars of equipment, received (at that time) less than $100,000 a year. The military, he told us, also had the fairest system of promotion of any large organization. According to Drucker, this was because the system minimized favoritism, nepotism, and other elements that discouraged promoting the best to positions of responsibility. He also said it did a much better job in leadership development.

Drucker believed that the best book on leadership was written almost two and a half millennia ago by Xenophon, a Greek general who had fought in Persia. In *Kyropaidaia* Xenophon wrote about leadership in battle. Thus, the "Father of Modern Management" recommended a book on combat leadership as the best book written on leadership for business leaders, simply because it taught good leadership.

Drucker spoke with such confidence and expertise about so many areas that I did not notice anything special about his use of military examples when I was his student, despite my own military background. However, as we talked more after my graduation from the Drucker School while I advanced in my Air Force career, I understood that Peter had a special interest in military leadership, much of which he strongly agreed with. The extent of his knowledge about the military, war, political relationships, and war's consequences was surprising. However, it is well to remember that Peter wrote for *Foreign Affairs* as well as the *Harvard Business Review*.

Drucker did not share the fact that he had this particular interest or knowledge with many people. However, it did come through occasionally in his writing. In a 1988 article on leadership in the *Wall Street Journal*, he cited Generals Eisenhower, Marshall, and MacArthur, Field Marshal Montgomery, and Julius Caesar—with little company from business leaders.[1]

Several years ago an article in *Fortune* magazine recommended military experience as the best leadership training for business. This opinion was shared by others. Richard Cavanaugh, president and CEO of the Conference Board, described a meeting of business leaders at a Manhattan restaurant. The panel, which apparently included Cavanaugh along with Drucker and Jack Welch, was asked: Who does the best job of developing leaders? To Cavanaugh's amazement, it was not the Harvard Business School, McKinsey and Company, or one of the great corporations that was cited as doing the best job. According to Cavanaugh, "The enthusiastic choice of both of these management legends was the United States military."[2]

A little later, Drucker's beliefs about the military received more publicity, mainly from Frances Hesselbein's books, *Hesselbein on Leadership* and *Be, Know, Do*, a book Hesselbein adapted from the official *Army Leadership Manual* and coauthored with General Eric K. Shinseki. Shinseki was a former army chief of staff forced into retirement by then Secretary of Defense Rumsfeld, when Shinseki testified before Congress and gave troop estimates needed for Iraq far above those planned by Rumsfeld. For the first time the extent to which Drucker both understood and approved of the military's unique mastery of leadership was publicized and well documented. In recommending Hesselbein's adaptation of the *Army Leadership Manual* on the dustcover of her book, Drucker wrote, "The Army trains and develops more leaders than do all other institutions together—and with a lower casualty rate."

CHAPTER 11

Leadership Lessons from Xenophon

Despite his many contributions to management, Drucker did not write much on leadership under the explicit title "leadership" until late in his career. The reason is partially explained in his first book focused entirely on management, *The Practice of Management*, published in 1954. In this book, Drucker wrote, "The first systematic book on leadership: the *Kyropaidaia* of Xenophon—himself no mean leader of men—is still the best book on the subject."[1]

Kyropaidaia is more than two thousand years old, but Drucker hadn't changed his mind twenty-five years later when I was his doctoral student. He told me he found *Kyropaidaia*, which goes by a number of titles in English, and another book by Xenophon, *Anabasis*, also known as *The Persian Expedition* and containing numerous leadership examples, "fascinating." Over years of study and writing, and despite all the books published on leadership by well-known academic researchers and successful CEOs, he did not alter his opinion. Xenophon was still the best.

Drucker felt that every single modern cutting-edge leadership concept had been described in these books: "The scores of books, papers and speeches on leadership in business enterprise that come out every year have little to say on the subject that was not already old when the Prophets spoke and Aeschylus wrote."[2] In other words, after Xenophon, little existed that hadn't been covered, and Xenophon's advice was still applicable for the modern business leader.

Drucker did come to believe that while there was nothing new, expressing this knowledge again in different ways was still beneficial. Toward the end of his career, Drucker realized that he himself had written much about leadership even though he almost never classified it as such.

Who Was Xenophon?

What was it about Xenophon that made the "Father of Modern Management" feel that his writings, above the work of all those writing on leadership, were the absolute best on the subject? In the fourth century B.C., Xenophon was a member of a 10,000-man Greek army hired by the pretender to the Persian throne, Cyrus the Younger, to defeat his brother. The Greeks were considered the best infantrymen in the world. Cyrus thought that with these trained mercenary troops he could defeat his brother's vastly superior force.

At first things went well, but in a crucial battle in Persia, Cyrus the Younger was killed. The Persians invited the Greek generals to a truce parley to discuss their withdrawal from Persia. All were to attend unarmed. However, this was a trap. As soon as they entered the Persian camp, they were cut off from any support and killed. The 10,000 leaderless Greeks were stranded in Babylon and surrounded by hostile forces. The Persians planned to kill them or sell them into slavery.

During a meeting to decide what to do, Xenophon was elected as one of the replacement generals and eventually the general-in-command. In *The Persian Expedition*, Xenophon tells the story of how he became the Greeks' commander and the fight to return to the Black Sea against overwhelming odds. This march, a story of courage, improvisation, discipline, self-sacrifice, and, above all, leadership—one of the most famous in ancient history—took five months.

After his return, Xenophon became a respected writer and historian, and, in *Kyropaidaia*, he described the leadership education of a famous Persian leader who had lived two hundred years earlier, Cyrus the Great. This chapter discusses some of the important leadership lessons you'll find written by Drucker's favorite leadership author in *Kyropaidaia* and *The Persian Expedition*.

The Consequences of Inaction

After the assassination of the Greek generals, there was considerable fear in the Greek camp. There was confusion and hesitation. Morale was low. Xenophon was not a general. He wasn't even a senior Greek officer. But no one was proposing action. All were just talking. They were above all, fearful. In their hearts, they knew that the Persians planned to kill as many of them as possible and sell the survivors into slavery, but they were afraid to admit it, even to themselves. Many wanted to meet with the Persians. They thought they could negotiate some sort of arrangement to save their lives.

Finally, Xenophon asked himself, "What am I doing here doing nothing? Am I waiting to become a little older? If I don't take action, I'll never become older—I'll be dead!"[3] He stepped forward and told his comrades that they had no hope in trying to negotiate. He told them that their enemies didn't want friendship or agreement. They wanted them dead or enslaved! He told them what needed to be done. He spoke convincingly and they elected him a general and overall commander.

This is a lesson for all leaders. There is never a reason for inaction. We must never take council of our fears, even when our fears are well founded. We must take whatever action is necessary, even if difficult and hazardous. As the saying goes, "Don't just stand there, do something!" Xenophon did.

Leading the Troops: Pointers for Subordinates

After becoming commander and creating subordinate generals, Xenophon called the new generals together and instructed them on leadership:[4]

1. Leaders set the example. If you are downhearted, your men will become cowards. If you are clearly prepared to meet the enemy and call on your soldiers to do their part, you can be sure they will try to emulate you.

2. Leaders need to be braver than those they lead, and must be the first to do hard work.

3. Leaders must be in control and exercise discipline, otherwise nothing useful ever gets done.

4. Leaders train their soldiers to think about positive action that each must take to be successful, otherwise they think about "what is going to happen to me?"

Xenophon walked his talk. When one soldier complained that he had to walk and carry a shield while Xenophon, though wearing a heavy cavalry breastplate, was mounted, Xenophon jumped from his horse, took the man's shield and pushed him out of the ranks. Xenophon led the pace and encouraged others while carrying the shield *and* wearing the heavy cavalry armor. When the going was light, he led on horseback; when the terrain was difficult or it was impossible to ride, he dismounted and led on foot from the front.[5]

When some of his soldiers were disheartened because the Greeks had few cavalry, and their enemies had many, Xenophon reminded them of something that centuries later, General George S. Patton told his army. "Wars may be fought with weapons, but they are won by men." Xenophon put it this way: "Ten thousand cavalry only amount to ten thousand men. No one has ever died in battle by being bitten or kicked by a horse; it is men who do whatever gets done in battle."[6]

The same is true of any human endeavor. Should your employees become despondent or overly concerned about your lack of resources compared to those of a competitor or about the situation they face, remember Xenophon. This doesn't mean that resources count for nothing; it does mean that they are not the deciding factor. People are. You can be successful without optimal resources, but not without good people. Xenophon took care of his people first. He kept his word to them and he never exploited his position for his own personal benefit. Just the opposite. When promises were made to his soldiers that were not fulfilled, Xenophon risked his own situation to ensure that promises made, even by others, were carried out. Moreover, he did this even after they returned to Greece and he personally was no longer commander and had little to gain.[7]

How to Motivate

Cyrus the Great of Persia was an absolute monarch. He held the power of life and death over his followers. He could reward or punish and motivate in any way he chose. As in many organizations, the carrot-and-stick approach was the norm at the time. But Cyrus chose not to motivate in this way. As Xenophon wrote in *Kyropaidaia*, Cyrus' father asked Cyrus what he thought was the best way to motivate his followers. Cyrus answered, "That which especially incites to obedience is the praising and honoring of one who obeys and the dishonoring of the one who disobeys."[8]

Cyrus' father agreed that one way to gain obedience was *by compulsion*, but he told Cyrus that there was a far superior way to get human beings to obey and "with great pleasure." Moreover, he told Cyrus that when people think that obedience will result in harm, they are not so ready to respond to the threat of punishment or to be seduced by gifts. This other method, which resulted in voluntary obedience, worked even when there was danger. In a business context, if the situation demands extraordinary work or risk, a worker may not respond to threats or promises of reward, either.

Cyrus' father explained that the method wasn't complicated. He only had to take care of his subordinates better than they took care of themselves, and to ensure that he took care of them even before himself in every situation. Who would not want to follow and obey a leader who looked to one's interest more than one would or could do personally? There is an old injunction in the military not to eat or sleep until one's soldiers have eaten and are bedded down. No doubt this was what Cyrus was taught. Maxwell Taylor, an American general and later adviser to President Kennedy and chairman of the Joint Chiefs of Staff, said, "A reflective reading of history will show that no man ever rose to military greatness who could not convince his troops that he put them first, above all else." Don't you think that employees in any company would feel the same way and support a leader and an organization that did this?

Reputation Must Be Earned

In another discussion, Cyrus asked his father how he could achieve a reputation for excellence and admiration as a leader as quickly as possible. Cyrus' father answered that there was no shortcut; reputation could be achieved only through learning, followed by a practical demonstration of his knowledge. It could not be achieved through what we call "office politics" or any form of self-promotion.[9]

It is interesting to note that another monarch, who also bore the title "the Great," followed the same advice. Peter I, the seventeenth Russian tsar, was called "the Great" for a reason. He not only was a great administrator and a great military leader, he founded the Russian empire, changing what had been a backward country into a modern Western state. Peter the Great served in every rank in the Russian army from private on up. Previous rulers received senior rank in an elite regiment or fleet even before they were teenagers. Peter refused to accept any rank he did not earn. He enlisted in the Preobrazhensky Regiment as a drummer boy because that was the very lowest position. He refused promotion, even when recommended by his commanders, until he felt he merited the promotion. And this was the future tsar!

When on garrison duty, or in the field, he permitted no distinction between himself and others. When it was his turn at guard duty, he performed that duty and any difficult or distasteful work, as did all Russian privates and in the same way. He slept in the same tents as his brother soldiers and ate the same food. When ordered to dig, he dug, and when the regiment paraded, he stood in the ranks, indistinguishable from those who would later be his subjects. As Cyrus' father explained and Xenophon documented, there is no substitute for leaders' knowing what they are talking about—none.

The Value of Worker Health in Leadership

Corporations over the last forty or fifty years have noted the advantages of keeping their employees healthy. They have gone far beyond health care by also providing workout facilities, time from work to exercise, and more. The Japanese have known this for far longer, and Americans who visited Japan during the Japanese management fad of the early 1980s were amazed to find that many, if not most, Japanese companies required group exercise of both their workers and managers every day.

Cyrus the Great knew the importance of having healthy troops more than two thousand years ago. His father told him: "Just as there are menders of torn clothes, so also these doctors whom you mention treat people after they get sick. But your concern for health must be more magnificent than this, for you need to be concerned that the army not get sick in the first place."[10] Cyrus implemented such policies as never allowing his men to come to lunch or dinner without first exercising them to the point of sweat. This was considered part of good leadership.[11]

Drucker's Thoughts on Xenophon

There are many other valuable lessons for corporate executives in Xenophon's writings. He practiced leadership in a different time and place and his challenges were different from those faced by most of us. Yet the concepts hold true today. Drucker understood this after reading and studying Xenophon's books. The basis of leadership about which Xenophon wrote, the lessons of his experiences, the principles of integrity, commitment, duty, and other concepts, are in no way altered by even the most recent research on leadership. Whatever the leadership challenges in whatever organization, much can be learned from Xenophon's experiences and writings.

I believe that Xenophon's books first caused Drucker to take a closer look at military leadership as practiced correctly, and eventually to recommend that it should be closely studied and applied by corporate and other leaders. The leadership described in Xenophon was consistently followed down through the ages to modern times. What follows is some slight evidence culled from the writings or pronouncements of senior military leaders. You can find hundreds of instructions over the millennia and from military practitioners from every country offering the same advice or examples as those found in Xenophon's books.

> Only after the men are settled in their encampment does the general retire; only after all the cooks have finished their cooking does he go in and eat.
> —*T'ai Kung Chiang Shang, ancient Chinese general*

I used to say to them, "go boldly in among the English," and then I used to go boldly in myself.
—*Joan of Arc, 1429–1430*

War must be carried on systematically, and to do it you must have men of character activated by principles of honor.
—*General George Washington, Commander Continental Army, 1776–1781*

A competent leader can get efficient service from poor troops, while on the contrary an incapable leader can demoralize the best of troops.
—*General of the Armies John J. Pershing, U.S. Army, 1917–1919*

Every Red Army commander must firmly grasp the fact that slavery to routine and extreme enthusiasm for some specific plan or some specific method are the most dangerous thing for all of us. . . . Nothing can be absolute or solidly fixed; everything flows and changes, and any means, any methods might be used in a certain situation.
—*General Mikhail V. Frunze, Soviet Army, Commander of the Eastern Front, 1919–1920*

You must not retain for one instant any man in a responsible position when you have become doubtful of his ability to do the job.
—*General of the Army Dwight D. Eisenhower, Supreme Allied Commander, Europe 1944–1945*

It is better to struggle with a stallion when the problem is how to hold it back, than to urge on a bull which refuses to budge.
—*Lieutenant General Moshe Dayan, Army of Israel, 1956–1957*

The principles of leadership in the military are the same as they are in business, in the church, and elsewhere: a. Learn your job. (This involves study and hard work.) b. Work hard at your job. c. Train your people. d. Inspect frequently to see that the job is being done properly.
—*Admiral Hyman G. Rickover, U.S. Navy, Father of the Nuclear Submarine*

We earn and sustain the respect and trust of the public and of our troops because of the integrity and self-discipline we demonstrate. Officers should strive to develop forthright integrity—officers who do the right thing in their professional and private lives—and have the courage to take responsibility for their choices.
—*General Ronald R. Fogleman, U.S. Air Force Chief of Staff 1995–1997*

Drucker recognized this consistency of leadership concepts in the military early in his career, and carried the belief that military leadership not only had it right, it had had it right for thousands of years, throughout his career. When asked to develop a presentation on leadership for a large bank in the late 1980s, he declined, explaining that although leadership was "all the rage," nothing about it was really new.[12]

Drucker on What Xenophon's Lessons Meant

- Most, if not all, concepts for effective and ethical leadership were documented by Xenophon in about 300 B.C.

- Military leadership in the twentieth and twenty-first centuries was based on and practiced the concepts Xenophon had written about more than two thousand years earlier.

- The military model of leadership (*not* to be confused with the notion that "business is war") had something for all organizational leaders.

CHAPTER 12

Training and Developing Leaders

In 1954, in his very first book specifically focused on management, Drucker wrote, "Leadership is of the utmost importance. Indeed there is no substitute for it." Unfortunately, in the same book and only a short few sentences later, he wrote, "Leadership cannot be taught or learned."[1] It took him more than forty years to change this opinion, and, in 1996, he demonstrated a complete reversal. In his foreword to *The Leader of the Future*, he wrote, "Leadership must be learned and can be learned."[2]

Although at first he believed leadership to be unlearnable, Drucker documented the importance of training right from the start. He fully understood that those he referred to as "knowledge workers" must be led. Years later, he came to appreciate that not only was leadership learnable, it was up to the organization to teach these skills. Even the best of universities could not do it—they could only teach theory, not practice. Drucker predicted that the focus of all learning would have to shift from the schools to employers and that every employer would have to take on this responsibility, which would include teaching leadership.[3]

Drucker was appalled by what was being done, or rather not being done in most corporations at that time. He considered their efforts at leadership development completely inadequate and contrasted them with what was being done in the nonprofit sector. He thought the lessons gained during World War II were extremely important, yet most companies largely ignored what the military had learned in the process of training people rapidly for jobs that could not have been anticipated only a short time earlier, and from training the leadership needed to manage a force that kept doubling and redoubling faster than any plan had ever envisioned.

Training Leaders in the Military and Civilian Worlds

There is an old saying in the military, possibly from Napoleon, that a marshal's baton can be found in every private's knapsack. Although today's privates do not carry knapsacks and the rank of marshal does not exist in the U.S. military, the principle behind these words still holds true. The primary reason is necessity. In battle, any leader, even a top commander, may become incapacitated—and when that happens a junior leader, or even a soldier not in a leadership role at all, must be prepared to immediately take charge, which includes responsibility for both mission accomplishment and for others' lives.

A remarkable incident from World War I illustrates the point. In the fall of 1918, Alvin York was a member of a seventeen-man American patrol led by a sergeant into the Argonne Forest in France. Behind enemy lines, a German machine gunner spotted the patrol, opened fire, and killed or wounded half of the patrol, including its leader. York took charge, and with the nine survivors destroyed thirty-five machine guns and captured well over a hundred German officers and men.

Of York's performance, the senior Allied commander, French Marshal Ferdinand Foch, said, "What you did was the greatest thing accomplished by any soldier of all the armies of Europe." York was promoted to sergeant and awarded the Congressional Medal of Honor, the nation's highest decoration. In 1941, he reluctantly agreed to a movie based on his diaries on condition that Gary Cooper played the lead. Cooper won a Best Actor Oscar for the role in *Sergeant York*.

What was all the fuss about? No one can deny York's heroism or the results obtained under his leadership. Yet, readiness to assume a leadership role is expected of every member of the military, who are generally trained for this.

Furthermore, it is not unheard of for individuals starting out at the bottom of the military career ladder to reach the top rungs. In recent years, General Johnnie Wilson entered the Army as a private, got his bachelor's degree, went to the Army's Officers Candidate School, and eventually rose to four-star general, the highest rank in the U.S. Army. General Alfred Gray entered the Marine Corps as a private, eventually became a four-star general and commandant of the Marines. Admiral Michael Boorda began his career as a lowly seaman, but beat the odds and wore the four stars of a full admiral as chief of naval operations. Eugene Habiger, an airman who was vice commander of an organization in which I once served, began as an infantry private, then left the Army and got a Bachelor of Science degree. He then enlisted in the Air Force, attended Air Force Officers Training School followed by flying school, and eventually became a four-star general and commander of the U.S. Strategic Command.

In a corporation, the equivalent would be if each of these men had started in the stockroom or mailroom and risen to CEO. This kind of advancement is rare in business, because most corporations do not see non-degreed new hires advancing very far. In fact, most professionals, even those with degrees or advanced degrees, do not become senior officers of the corporations they enter, nor are they expected to do so. Only a few are identified early as up-and-comers and put in positions where they get the experience necessary for promotion to high positions. Leadership training, as such, is rare for new hires regardless of their backgrounds or degrees.

Leadership Training: Starting on Day One

Because every member of the military must be ready to assume leadership responsibilities and to lead effectively without delay or additional instruction, leadership training begins on the very first day of basic training. This is done by example, and continues for as long as the individual remains in the military. Even senior officers are continually given leadership training of some sort.

Most corporations fail to give leadership training until it is perceived to be needed; that is, pending new responsibilities. Some corporations have developed excellent leadership training and development programs, but these tend to be at the mid to higher levels, not for newly hired professionals, and certainly not for new stockroom employees and the equivalent. The one exception to this no-training practice is for what Drucker called "crown princes," about whom I'll talk shortly.

Focus on Performance, Not Potential

In the military, leaders are selected and groomed for greater leadership based on their performance, not the potential they appeared to show on entry. For example, a cohort of "new hire professionals" is commissioned at the lowest officer rank each year. They come from a variety of sources: ROTC, officer training or candidate schools, and the service academies: the U.S. Military Academy (West Point), the Naval Academy, and the Air Force Academy. What happens afterward is largely based on their performance, not where they came from. General Curtis LeMay was chief of staff of the Air Force when most general officers of the Army and the Air Force had attended West Point. General LeMay had not. He graduated from Ohio State University. Queried by an ROTC cadet about chances for advancement given the high percentage of West Point generals, LeMay said, "It never hurt me any."

Table 12.1 details figures on commission sources for a recent year.[4] Direct appointments are for specialists such as physicians, dentists, chaplains, and attorneys, who are treated differently, but strictly within their specialty. The Marine Corps figure is relatively low in direct appointments because they rely on the Navy for officers in medical and dental specialties and chaplains, which lowers their need for direct commissioning. "Other" refers to officers trained in one service but commissioned in another, for example, commissioning from West Point to, say, the Air Force. Only a limited number are permitted, usually on a one-for-one exchange with the gaining service academy, and on a volunteer basis. All officers are treated identically regardless of the source of their commissioning.

Similarly, Drucker pointed out that there should be no "crown princes" in business, anointed because they were graduates of

Table 12.1—Sources of Commission

Source of Commission by Percentage	Army	Navy	Marine Corps	Air Force
Academy	15.5	20.6	16.2	18.2
ROTC–scholarship	36.3	20.6	2.4	2.4
ROTC–No scholarship	17.1	1.8	0.0	35.4
OCS or OTS	13.6	19.3	60.9	21.8
Direct appointment	11.5	18.0	0.6	18.4
Other	5.9	*	0.0	1.1
Unknown	0.1	19.8	19.9	2.9
Total**	100.0	100.1	100.0	100.2

Notes: *Less than 0.1 percent.

**Totals for the Navy and Air Force are slightly off due to rounding errors.

prestigious MBA programs or for some other reason and identified on hire for special treatment.[5] Drucker noted, "My experience is that the correlation between the high-promise people at age twenty-three and the performers at forty-five is very poor."[6]

Although a number of appointees to officer rank, in addition to the specialists, have advanced degrees, even doctorates from prestigious schools, they all begin at the same level and receive essentially the same opportunities and treatment. West Point did a study of cadets some years ago that attempted to predict later rank as officers. Moderate academic grades coupled with somewhat above-average athletic performance seemed to lead to higher rank. However, even these results weren't statistically significant.

Critics will point out exceptions, and the rule of no "crown princes" in the military was not always true. I mentioned earlier the high percentage of West Point generals in the first part of the twentieth century. At one point, something like 85 percent of the U.S. Army's generals were West Point graduates. None other than often-deprecated Major General George Armstrong Custer, speaking against the formation of an association of West Point graduates, said: "I stand second to none about my being proud of being a West Point graduate, but to encourage elitism in the officer corps based on the fact of being a graduate of West Point is unfair and stupid." The Association of Graduates of the United States Military Academy was formed anyway, but the Army and the military in general has managed to avoid the "crown prince" syndrome in recent years.

The Need for Continual Evaluation and Feedback

In the military, the learning of leadership is a lifetime process. One does not take a course and then move on to entirely new things. Drucker learned from his association with Japanese companies that continual introduction of new concepts was not sufficient to maximize productivity. Rather, increased productivity requires continual training, and the greatest benefit of leadership training—in fact any training—is not learning the new, but learning to do better what is already known.[7] He thought that the Japanese had learned this from the Zen masters, and recommended that this philosophy be adopted for training. Drucker even criticized early but well-accepted management theorists Frederick Taylor and Elton Mayo for not better teaching what was already known. He believed that continuous training creates receptivity for the new, the different, the innovative, the more productive.[8] In other words, it is a precursor for development.

This is precisely the military approach to developing leaders. The subject is never abandoned and continual study and development is expected. Leadership training is conducted at all levels of management. Moreover, leadership potential and performance is evaluated throughout an individual's career, and face-to-face feedback on leadership performance is provided after every evaluation. This is typically done annually, as well as on reassignment to a different unit or to a supervisor.

In Peter's view, high-level training of this type, including a review of the performance of boards of directors, was essential. He wrote that few corporations do what the larger nonprofits do routinely: put new board members through systematic training.[9]

Applied and Practical Training

Leadership training in the military is not limited to coursework; it is also accomplished through doing. Every leader is expected to develop the leadership of subordinates by giving them opportunities to lead, if only temporarily. While leaders do not allow those tested and taught in this manner to cause permanent harm to the organization or to have a negative impact on the accomplishment of its mission, they do allow them to make mistakes. This is essential. As Drucker wrote, "Work as a lieutenant or assistant does not adequately prepare a man for making his own decisions." He goes on to say that it is essential that in addition to regular training, the individual must be tested.[10]

In the military, this practical training is accomplished partially by rotating job assignments. This can be done both by shifting people to different jobs at one geographic location and by a permanent change of assignment to a new organization at a new location every few years. The military is fortunate in having a sufficiently large organization to do this smoothly and the ability to shift a few people at a time so as not to disrupt the organization. Some companies do this today, but often it is in connection with "crown princes" identified as up-and-comers, who are sometimes hired into a planned program of assignment rotation. While this aids in the leadership development of those in these special programs, it is far different from the applied and practical training given everyone in the military.

The Importance of Follow-Through

One of the biggest differences in leadership between the military and elsewhere is that all members of a military organization are taught from the very beginning that it is not enough to issue an order or to give instructions, but that in every case the leader must follow through to ensure that these instructions are carried out. Drucker said even military writers in ancient times such as Xenophon, Thucydides, and Caesar took this for granted, as did the earliest Chinese texts on military arts.[11] It was not something new. It was simply taught and done routinely in the military, but not always outside of it.

How to Handle Mistakes

After I joined the civilian workforce, I was amazed how frequently individuals were terminated for frivolous reasons, sometimes things not the individual's fault. On his first day, a new engineer was fired on the spot for making an error that cost the company a lot of money, although he carried out the orders exactly as given him by the chief engineer. The chief engineer had not communicated accurately what he wanted done, and compounded his error by not checking back to ascertain that it was being done correctly. In contrast, a leader like Thomas Watson, founder of IBM, is rare. On one occasion, a new vice president made an error that cost IBM $1,000,000, at a time when that was "real money." Ordered to Watson's office, the vice president thought he would be fired. "Fire you?" bellowed Watson. "We just paid a million dollars to educate you."

Individuals are accountable in the military, but not until they have been properly trained. Moreover, firing is rare and usually only for major mistakes; furthermore, "firing" usually means reassignment, not dismissal from the military. Major General Lloyd Fredendall did such a poor job commanding the Army's II Corps at the Battle of Kasserine Pass during World War II that he was relieved of command and replaced by another major general—George S. Patton. Fredendall was not considered a good combat commander and he was returned to the States where he held a number of training assignments.

Drucker always said the "Peter Principle" (referring to Lawrence J. Peter, not Peter Drucker) was nonsense. The Peter Principle held that one rose to the level of one's incompetence, which ended the person's career. Peter, Drucker that is, believed that an individual could be inept at one kind of job and yet brilliant in another. Fredendall was a case in point. He proved to be so outstanding in his training jobs that he eventually commanded the Second U.S. Army, a training organization, and was promoted to lieutenant general, from two-star to three-star rank.

Advantages of the Military Model

Because so many leaders are trained and developed, a much larger pool of leaders exists for selection to any leadership position in the military than in civilian organizations. Moreover, the transition to a position of leadership and higher responsibility is usually much easier in the military than in the civilian world. Because of job rotation, there is more flexibility when important posts become available, and a better understanding of what other positions in the organization entail. Moreover, while there is an intense desire to do well, and definite accountability, mistakes can sometimes be more easily forgiven in military versus civilian ranks.

Without sufficient training in the duties of higher office, some would-be leaders might look mainly at the privileges rather than the problems and headaches of higher rank. Training and leadership experience tend to dampen this expectation so that future leaders see both the pluses and minuses of holding future higher responsibilities.

The continued emphasis on training and improving leadership skills gives an organization's members tools and the ability to apply them. Like the Zen masters referred to by Drucker, the organization's leaders are on a continuous track of improvement. They get better and better. I've written several books about applying these techniques to civilian endeavors. One was subtitled "Dare the Impossible; Achieve the Extraordinary." A review of the actions military leaders are sometimes required to perform daily makes a good case for this description of military leadership.

Drucker on Training and Developing Leaders

Although the concepts are not complicated and are doable, adapting them requires an investment, but more than that, a firm commitment. As Peter said, "What do we know about developing people? Quite a bit." He cautioned not to focus only on skills for the immediate future, but to build for the leader's entire career and life. He emphasized that mentoring and training, both theoretical and practical, are critical in that they focus on what the developing leader is doing right rather than what has been done wrong. He said to avoid "the crown prince syndrome" described previously. He quoted the pastor of a church from which many successful leaders had emerged, who tried to provide four things to newly developing leaders:

- A mentor for guidance

- A teacher to develop skills

- A judge to evaluate progress

- An encourager to cheer them on[12]

This is a good description of how the military develops leaders, and how any organization can and should develop them as well.

CHAPTER 13

Promotion and Staffing

Without the right people, no organization can be very effective. Good leaders are a multiplier of effectiveness and efficiency—and poor leaders have exactly the opposite effect. Therefore, a single leader affects the performance of many others and the promotion of the right people and the staffing of an organization, especially its leadership positions, is of particular importance. Drucker called these "life and death decisions" and wrote in depth about them.

The individual most to be emulated according to Drucker was General George C. Marshall, chief of staff of the U.S. Army during World War II and later secretary of state. He greatly admired Marshall's attention to detail, and his early identification (even before he rose to chief of staff) of up-and-comers along with their strengths and weaknesses. Perhaps the most outstanding example of Marshall's system of staffing was General, later President, Dwight D. Eisenhower. Drucker also applauded Marshall's willingness to sacrifice his own ambitions for the greater good, as when Marshall gave Eisenhower command of the greatest seaborne invasion in the history of the world while Marshall remained in his own less glamorous but high-level staff position in Washington, which he felt was more important for winning the war. As noted in Chapter Twelve, though Drucker recognized its imperfections, he commended the attributes that made up the U.S. military's system of promotion and staffing.

Before examining Drucker's views on promotion and staffing, I need to distinguish between the two components of promotion and staffing, which are not necessarily synonymous. Promotion influences, but does not necessarily determine, who should be selected for an executive job, whereas staffing is the selection of an individual to fill a particular job vacancy. Both are crucial aspects of putting the right people in the right positions for success of the organization.

Promotion can be in rank, title, compensation, position, benefits, status, or privileges, but it may or may not involve an actual change of assignment to a particular *position* (staffing). Promotion in rank or title by itself may make an individual *eligible* for a more significant position, but does not guarantee it. I present a specific example of this later in the chapter.

In the military, different insignias of rank make the distinction between individuals obvious. However this isn't only done in the military. Some companies require employees to wear security badges with different color schemes indicating progressively higher rank from line worker and basic professional through manager, senior manager, assistant director, director, vice president, and president. Mary Kay Cosmetics has a system of representing higher levels of achievement through items of clothing and what is worn on them, culminating in a complete outfit. Paintings of the women who have achieved the top levels, "in uniform," are on display at headquarters in Dallas, Texas.[1]

A Rational Promotion System

Peter argued strongly for a rational system of promotion. He recognized that undeserved promotion not only resulted in higher incidences of failure and mediocrity, it also tremendously de-motivated both those more deserving who were passed over and those who simply observed dysfunctional management promotion decisions. He cautioned against two common errors: promotion to get rid of someone performing poorly and failure to promote someone considered indispensable in a current position. Finally, he listed several characteristics of a rational system:

- Consideration of all eligibles, not just those highly visible

- Consideration of all functional backgrounds

- Normal promotion from within, but consideration of desirable outsiders[2]

The third characteristic applies more to staffing than promotion, but Drucker did not distinguish here between the two.

Drucker noted additional criteria for a rational promotion system, although he did not identify them as such. The first was that neither promotion nor staffing should be in the hands of a single individual. Yet in most companies, except at the highest levels of the organization, this is exactly what is done. Drucker's argument was that there is no safeguard against bias, faulty, or arbitrary judgment, which a rational system of promotion should have.[3] However it also helps to explain his interest in the military promotion system, which I explain in the following section.[4]

The Military Promotion System

Drucker thought that the systems used for promotion selection in the U.S. military, while not perfect, were the fairest and probably the best used by any large organization. As he said, "The Army trains and develops more leaders than do all other organizations together—and with a lower casualty rate."[5] If you compare the U.S. military's system with Drucker's criteria for a rational system, it is easy to see why he favored it.

While there are some differences among the U.S. military services, they are relatively minor. At most levels, promotion is based strictly on merit, that is, proven performance. Beginning at the junior noncommissioned officer ranks through the rank of major general, promotion boards meet and decide on who will be promoted. In most cases, the boards are very competitive and promote on a "best qualified" basis. For example, there usually are several thousand colonels vying for a handful of promotions to brigadier general, so the promotion rate may be something like 1 or 2 percent. At the junior noncommissioned officer and junior officer levels, promotion may be on a "fully qualified basis," which means that all who have performed satisfactorily are considered qualified and promoted. Usually failure of an officer to win a promotion after several opportunities entails discharge from the military.

For the top two ranks, lieutenant general and general, and for the naval services vice admiral and admiral (those whose insignias of rank are three and four stars, respectively), there are no promotion boards. Candidates are nominated for specific jobs, and if selected are promoted to one of these two highest ranks. This is where promotion and staffing in the military are linked.

Written Appraisals

Many companies require various types of evaluation or appraisal reports. Drucker's problem with them was that they are rarely used for promotion.[6] The main tool for promotion selection in the military is the evaluation report. While these reports vary somewhat among the services, and for officers versus enlisted ranks, they typically involve evaluation on a number of specific criteria. For example, the current Army form involves a written evaluation of an officer's ability in communicating, decision making, motivating, planning, executing, assessing, developing, team building, and learning. Many service evaluations require specific examples of performance. They also ask for an overall evaluation of potential for promotion at that time and frequently some sort of ranking of where the individual rated stands compared with others of the same rank being evaluated.

Usually, the rater's supervisor must add a personal endorsement and comments, especially an agreement or disagreement with the evaluation and the reasons for either reaction. If the evaluation is especially good or especially poor, the rater's supervisor's supervisor must also get into the act and add an endorsement. The evaluation is discussed with the individual rated before forwarding. Currently, at least one of the services requires quarterly counseling regarding progress made after the annual evaluation.

Over time, variations of this system have been tried. In an effort to control evaluation inflation, that is, a rater giving all subordinates a high rating, the Air Force at one point required raters to assign those rated a 1, 2, or 3 score, 1 being the highest. However, raters were severely restricted in the number of 1's they could assign depending on the number of subordinates they rated. This procedure was discontinued because it was found to be unfair for many and counterproductive. For example, an elite all-volunteer unit might have all top people and all actually performing at a 1 level. Yet, if the group was small, few, if any, 1's could be awarded. So a 2 or even a 3 evaluation awarded in such an organization might describe performance that could be awarded a 1 elsewhere.

Other variations are at the general officer level where a so-called closed form is used, and, in some services, there is no formal evaluation counseling session. The rating is limited to a few short sentences—or even a single sentence—regarding the general's performance, and the ratee may or may not see the report. At that level, you are working for the next higher-ranking general anyway, and it is thought that after passing all the screens and achieving the rank of general officer, formal written feedback probably won't do much to improve performance or change or improve any personal quirks or deficiencies. The rated general's boss either likes or does not like the way the subordinate general is operating.

If a subordinate is performing poorly, the rater can take action to have the individual removed from the current position, in combat or in a critical noncombat role, immediately—even if the subordinate has done nothing illegal or immoral and has not violated the Uniform Code of Military Justice (military law) in any way. Normally someone relieved of duties in this way will automatically receive a bad evaluation, and these are difficult, but not impossible, to recover from. Colin Powell describes how he made some mistakes and received a poor rating in one assignment as a brigadier general.[7] Nevertheless, he went on to become a four-star general and chairman of the Joint Chiefs of Staff, the highest-ranking officer in the U.S. military. In addition, a bad appraisal can be contested, and a board may agree and expunge it from the individual's file. While infrequent, this does happen.

Getting Promoted

Not everyone is eligible for promotion to the next higher rank at every year's promotion. This generally has to do with the amount of time in the rank held or total years of service, or both, and this may change depending on the needs of the service at that time. During the years between World Wars I and II, Eisenhower held the rank of major for sixteen years (1920 to 1936), not because he performed poorly, but rather because the U.S. Army shrank after its rapid growth during the First World War. At the time, Eisenhower didn't have enough years of total service to be considered for promotion to the next higher grade, lieutenant colonel. While required time in grade varies by service, today a major (the Navy rank equivalent is lieutenant commander) is normally considered for promotion to lieutenant colonel (the navy rank of commander) at the sixteenth year of commissioned service, although a few may be selected for what is called a "below the zone" promotion a year or two earlier. Since Eisenhower was commissioned in 1915, based on the Army's current needs, he would have been eligible for early promotion to lieutenant colonel in 1929 instead of 1936.

The first step in being promoted is meeting a promotion board. Even though all are trained and qualified for promotion, not all can be promoted. The number holding each rank in each service is limited by law. At the officer ranks (beginning with second lieutenant in the Air Force, Army, and Marines, and ensign in the Navy and Coast Guard), those failing to be promoted usually are given several attempts. Should they not succeed, they are usually required to leave the service. This policy is known as "up or out." It helps to ensure a young force and the highest-quality personnel at every level.

The number that can be promoted in any one year depends on need and the policies at the time. According to recent figures in the Army, the promotion rate to lieutenant colonel is about 70 percent of those eligible and meeting the board. This may vary by both time and service. I have seen promotion to the rank of major much lower than 40 percent, and to lieutenant colonel, lower yet in the Air Force at different times. It all depends on the situation and the number that can be promoted. It probably was even lower than these figures when Eisenhower was promoted to these ranks.

The higher the promotion, the more difficult it is to attain. Promotion to colonel is much more difficult, and to general tougher yet. A retired Air Force four-star general once told forty newly promoted brigadier generals, of which I was one, lest we be too full of ourselves, "The Air Force could have reached into our pot of several thousand eligible colonels and pulled out forty other names at random, not yours. Can you imagine the effect on our ability to perform our mission successfully over the next five years? Most likely, none at all." It was an accurate but sobering thought, which made us realize that while gaining promotion was something to be proud of, we had some highly qualified competitors and we were all replaceable.

The Promotion Board

The promotion board is made up of people more senior than those being considered for promotion and from various units throughout the particular service. The same individuals usually do not sit on successive boards.

Promotion boards consider everything: past performance as demonstrated by written evaluation reports based mainly on demonstrated performance, types of experience, education (both degrees and professional military), awards and decorations, anything else positive and negative, and other things the promotion board might be instructed to give special weight to, such as combat duty.

No one, no matter how senior, not even the chief of staff of the service involved, can get a favorite officer promoted directly. This is considered "undue influence," and everyone involved can get in serious trouble. I remember the commander of Strategic Air Command, a four-star general bemoaning the fact that he knew some particular captain personally, and though he felt that this individual should be promoted to major, there was little he could do to except recommend him in his performance evaluation. Another four-star general, an Air Force chief of staff, was questioned by the secretary of defense regarding the selection for promotion to major general of a particular general the secretary did not want promoted. "Why did you select him for promotion?" the secretary demanded. "Sir, it is not the chief's promotion board. It is the Air Force's promotion board and the Air Force selected him," was the chief's response.

The promotion board reviews the records of everyone eligible. The board members may do this in three committees of three, or a total of nine on the board. Each committee scores each candidate's performance and record, say on a 1–7 basis, 7 being the highest, and compares scores on each candidate. If the score of a candidate by one committee differs by more than two points from another committee, that entire board discusses the candidate until consensus is reached. In my experience, a difference of more than two points is rare and affects only a very small percentage of the candidates reviewed. The board then ranks all candidates according to their numerical scores and further ranks them within the point scores achieved. Promotion decisions then depend on the number that can be made.

Officer selections might be screened further, especially at the general officer level, which, in accordance with the law, must be confirmed by the U.S. Senate. The Senate is not a rubber stamp; it has blocked promotions for various reasons, as has the secretary of defense. Of course, the system is not perfect, and mistakes are sometimes made both in promotion and nonpromotion, but everything possible is done to ensure fairness. It is easy to see why Drucker liked the system, since it met his basic criterion of a rational promotion system very well.

Promotion, however, is not staffing. It merely makes a candidate eligible for a higher-level position. It does not necessarily mean that an individual will be selected for a specific position. An Army battalion of eight hundred to a thousand individuals is typically commanded by an officer holding the rank of lieutenant colonel. However, the Army has far more lieutenant colonels than battalions, so many are not selected to command battalions. They do other jobs. Similarly an officer may be selected to command a battalion, yet for various reasons not promoted to the rank of lieutenant colonel. In the *Band of Brothers* TV series, based on the real history of Easy Company, 506th Parachute Regiment in the 101st Airborne Division during World War II, Major Dick Winters, former Easy Company commander and then battalion executive officer (second in command), is appointed to command the battalion. However, he remains a major and is not given the rank of lieutenant colonel while in this position as battalion commander.

Where Drucker Differed with the Military System

Drucker did differ significantly with the military system in one aspect, which had more to do more with staffing than promotion. The military, and many civilian organizations as well, use something known as "the whole man concept." That is, everything about an individual is considered when promotion decisions are made. Drucker opposed using this concept for promotion because he knew that frequently great leaders also suffered from great faults or weaknesses. He stated that promoting based on the absence of faults as opposed to the ability to do the job led only to mediocrity.

Staffing Decisions

Drucker did not cling to old thoughts as his thinking developed. This can easily be seen in his thoughts on staffing. In a chapter titled "Staffing for Excellence" in his book *People and Performance* (published in 1977), he discusses three rules for effective staffing.[8] However, by the time his updated version of *The Effective Executive* appeared in 2004, this list had grown to four rules:[9]

- Guard against "the impossible job." Any job that has defeated two or three individuals who had proven themselves in their previous assignments must be redesigned.

- Make jobs demanding and big.

- Start with what an individual can do and not what the job requires. Thus, the need for appraisals. (This was the rule added in the ensuing twenty-five years.)

- Finally, his primary rule: Staff for the single strength needed and be willing to put up with weakness.

He stated this fourth point repeatedly in his writings, and liked to cite the story of Grant, who had been cashiered out of the "old Army" prior to the Civil War because of his drinking and was said to have started drinking again during the war. Lincoln's response to this news, "Find out his brand so I may send it to all my generals."

Drucker suggested decision steps to help leaders in their staffing decisions. These too were increased from what he had taught in class ten years earlier:[10]

1. Think through the assignment so that you understand what needs to be done.
2. Look at a number of potentially qualified people.
3. Decide who can actually do the job best, ignoring irrelevant weaknesses.
4. Discuss each of the candidates with several people who have actually worked with them.
5. Make certain that the appointee understands the job.

Drucker on Promotion and Staffing

- Institute a rational promotion system, which includes all eligible for promotion.

- Don't just issue appraisals, use them for promotion.

- Promote using a board, not the opinions of one person.

- Staff for the strength required for the job, not to avoid weaknesses that are not relevant to the job.

- Discuss candidates for a job with those they have worked with.

- Make certain that the appointee understands the job.

CHAPTER 14

The Heart of Leadership

I n the introduction to Part Three, I talk about Drucker's thoughts on military leadership—some carefully concealed, others explicit from his very early writings—until the 2000s when he boldly claimed the military's training and development of leaders as preeminent in both quality and quantity over all other institutions.[1] However, for me the confirmation of his point of view was not his words in the classroom, those written in his books, or even this strong testimonial for military leadership in Frances Hesselbein's book. Rather, it came from a discussion we had over lunch in an Italian restaurant in Claremont, California. I'll get to that shortly.

Command-and-Control Leadership

Conventional wisdom is that military leadership is command-and-control leadership, and that it is an outdated style to be avoided. As Drucker liked to say, "What everyone knows is frequently wrong." While the term "command and control" is used in the military, there is no such thing in the military as command-and-control leadership. Command and control is the exercise of authority and direction over assigned forces by a commander to accomplish a mission. In other words, a commander is responsible for accomplishing a task and has the legal authority to issue orders that are enforceable by law. However, this is not leadership, and it doesn't refer to how a commander goes about exercising that authority. Simply giving orders is not leadership. In fact, very effective leadership in the military is frequently accomplished by taking the opposite tack and not giving orders at all. I learned this when I was still in high school.

A classmate's grandfather was a retired army major general. As a senior, I was very proud of my exalted status as a cadet lieutenant, and proud to be invited to a school basketball game with my classmate and his grandfather. After enjoying a candy bar purchased for me by the general, I surreptitiously (or so I thought) attempted to dispose of the wrapper by dropping it between the bleachers on which we sat. I knew it was wrong, but I didn't want to leave the stands and miss the action while locating a trash barrel. Unfortunately, the general did notice the action I was about to take. He didn't give me an order, he said only, "You know, although I hate to hang on to trash, but sometimes we have to, because throwing it away sets a very bad example for children." I'm sure my face turned red. That I remember this incident more than fifty years later says a lot about the effectiveness of indirect criticism as a leadership technique. I have frequently seen and used indirect methods in the military, even though I had the authority to simply give a direct order.

Leadership in Battle

Battle leadership probably represents one of the greatest leadership challenges. Pressure is severe, life is terribly hazardous, and working conditions are poor. There is probably greater uncertainty than in any other type of human activity. Drucker noted, "In no other type of leadership must the leader make decisions based on less or less reliable information."[2] "Workers" may need to perform their duties with little food and irregular sleep. All must take great risks. Most—followers and leaders alike—would prefer to be somewhere else doing something else.

Even then, an indirect approach can be used. During World War I, General Douglas MacArthur, then a thirty-eight-year-old brigadier general, had been in combat for some time, but had just assumed command of a new brigade in France. After planning an important attack, he went forward and waited in the trenches with the battalion that was going to lead the way. This battalion had never been in combat, much less made an attack. He could see that the young battalion commander was nervous.

He called the battalion commander to him. "Major," he addressed him, "when the signal comes to attack, if you get out in front of your battalion, your men will follow you all the way to the German positions. Moreover, they will never doubt your leadership or courage in the future."

Normally, a battalion commander is not supposed to lead an attack from the front. The military tactics manuals said that a battalion commander should be with the company that follows the company in the lead, not in front of the entire battalion. That way, the battalion commander is not as vulnerable and can better control the attack as it unfolds. But MacArthur knew that there was a time when the rules must be violated, and that this was one.

"I will not order you to do this," continued MacArthur. "In front of your battalion, many German guns will be aimed right at you. It will be very dangerous and require a great deal of courage. However, if you do it, your battalion will succeed. You will earn the Distinguished Service Cross [an award second only to the Congressional Medal of Honor] for your bravery, and I will see that you get it."

MacArthur then stepped back a few paces and looked the major up and down. He then stepped up to the major again. "I see you are going to do it," he said. "So, you will have the Distinguished Service Cross right now." Whereupon MacArthur unpinned one of his own Distinguished Service Crosses from his uniform and pinned it on the uniform of the major.

Of course, the major, proudly wearing the Distinguished Service Cross (which he had not yet actually earned), charged out in front of his troops. And, as MacArthur had forecast, his troops followed behind him. As a result, they succeeded in securing their objective.[3]

While there are true military geniuses in battle, the vast majority, as in most organizations, are ordinary men and women. Many are not professionals. Not all are suited to their jobs. Professional or amateur, all are stressed far more than in any civilian situation or occupation. Moreover, leaders must not only carry out the mission but also do their best to protect the lives of those they lead. For this reason, battle probably represents a worst-case scenario. No wonder traditional motivators such as high pay, good benefits, and job security aren't much good when it comes to motivating the troops. There is no "business as usual" on the battlefield.

Why Emulate Military Leadership?

As noted earlier, to some unfamiliar with it, military leadership is not something to emulate. It seems to involve running around shouting orders as in a Hollywood movie or obeying the foolish orders of someone in authority. Most who have been there know better. Sure, as in any organization, there are combat leaders who do a poor job of leading, operating as martinets and providing the models for what popular culture asserts is the way all military leaders lead.

However, the vast majority of combat leaders are not of that mold. Instead, they enable ordinary people to routinely accomplish the extraordinary. In battle, leaders help their followers to reach very difficult goals and complete very arduous tasks. Conditions of leadership in battle represent the worst that any leader might encounter. Peter said, "People cannot be managed; they must be led." In battle, they are led, and despite the terrible conditions, successful combat leaders build amazing organizations that accomplish their tasks ethically, honestly, and, for the most part, humanely.

Applying Battle Leadership to Organizational Leadership

Although I appreciated the value of what I personally learned about leadership in battle—it formed the basis of most of the recommendations in my first book on leadership in 1989—I wondered whether there were underlying principles or lessons from warfare that were at the root of all leadership success. It was the Bible, specifically the prophets Isaiah and Micah, that spoke of beating swords into ploughshares. Certainly this is a worthy goal. And if general principles of leadership from the worst-case scenario of warfare could be uncovered, leaders from all organizations could use these principles to dramatically increase productivity and the likelihood of success in any project. This would be the heart of leadership.

Swords into Ploughshares

The foundation of my research was a survey sent to more than two hundred former combat leaders and conversations with hundreds more. I asked what they had learned from leadership in battle. I asked about the tactics they used, about the importance of their style and the most important actions a leader must take. I asked about adapting these lessons to their civilian careers. I especially sought those who had become successful in the corporate world or in other nonmilitary organizations after leaving the armed forces. Among the responses I received in the initial phase, sixty-two were from generals and admirals.

I found that while they practiced many different styles of leadership, they followed some universal principles to dramatically boost productivity and achieve extraordinary success in all types of organizations. With so many respondents listing three or more principles, I expected a huge list. Napoleon developed and published 115 maxims on the conduct of war. How many hundreds of leadership principles would I uncover after analyzing and tabulating the input from such a large number of respondents?

Surprisingly, I discovered that 95 percent of the responses I received boiled down to only eight principles. Moreover, each of these leaders had seen one or more of these eight principles help them to achieve extraordinary results outside the military. More than a few wrote special notes or letters to express their support for my project. It was as if they had seen payment in blood for what they had learned. They knew its value, and they didn't want to see it wasted.

In a later phase of my research, I interviewed other successful senior business and organization leaders and reviewed dozens of corporate situations and the actions of their senior leaders. Some had combat backgrounds. Some did not. Some allowed me to use their real names and companies. Some preferred to remain anonymous. Some had developed their own lists of principles of leadership over the years. While their lists differed, they invariably included the eight I had previously developed.

I decided that these were far more than principles; they were actually universal laws of leadership—the heart of leadership. There are hundreds of excellent techniques and rules that people may follow in leading others, but these eight are essential. I believe they are the very essence of all leadership. Although these eight laws are simple, even one of them can make the difference between the success and failure in any project in any organization. You can make many mistakes and still succeed as a leader, but if you violate these universal laws, you will probably fail, even if you are at first successful. No one can guarantee success, because other factors might override anything a leader may be able to do, but there is no question that if you follow the universal laws, your chances of success are much increased.

I believe that these laws are that powerful and that the consequences of following them can be the determining factor in the success of most leaders in most situations. The eight laws are:

1. Maintain absolute integrity.

2. Know your stuff.

3. Declare your expectations.

4. Show uncommon commitment.

5. Expect positive results.

6. Take care of your people.

7. Put duty before self.

8. Get out in front.

In the fall of 1997, I shared this information with Peter. This was at the Italian restaurant in Claremont that I mentioned at the opening of the chapter. Peter wore hearing aids that could be adjusted individually for ambient sounds. In the restaurant environment it was sometimes difficult to be understood. But he made certain that he understood exactly what I was saying and that he grasped the results I had obtained from my research. He was very enthusiastic about the project and encouraged me in my desire to publish my research in an applied volume for managers. The resulting book was *The Stuff of Heroes: The Eight Universal Laws of Leadership*.[4]

Drucker and the Eight Principles

To give you some idea of Drucker's feelings about leadership in this regard, I will share his responses to each "law" at the time I shared them with him, which I have reconstructed from notes I scribbled at the time. I have since found written references by Drucker that confirm his responses to each "universal law." In each case, I have cited only one reference, although there were sometimes many.

Jim Collins, author of the mega best seller, *Good to Great*,[5] told Ira Jackson, dean of the Peter F. Drucker and Masatoshi Ito Graduate School of Management, that his book, based on extensive research, could have been called "Drucker Was Right." After locating these references and reading what Drucker had written, I felt the same about my own research.

I. Integrity First

"You are entirely right and absolutely correct in listing this as your first law. A leader can be well-liked and popular and even competent and that's all well and good, but if he lacks integrity of character he is not fit to be a leader."

Drucker wrote: "They [followers] may forgive a man a great deal: incompetence, ignorance, insecurity or bad manners. But they will not forgive him lack of integrity."[6]

2. Know Your Stuff

"This seems obvious, but some managers do try to cut corners rather than mastering the knowledge that they must have and that is essential to the quality of their performance."

Drucker wrote: "Leadership rests on being able to do something others cannot do at all or find difficult to do.[7]

3. Declare Your Expectations

"I'm uncertain what you mean by this. If you mean that a leader should declare his objectives, his mission—by all means."

Drucker wrote: "Each manager, from the 'big boss' down to the production foreman or the chief clerk, needs clearly spelled out objectives. . . . A statement of his own objectives based on those of the company and of the manufacturing department should be demanded even of the foreman on the assembly line."[8]

4. Show Uncommon Commitment

"The failure of many is because they show no commitment, or commitment to the wrong goals. This gets back to your third law. Commitment comes from a worthy mission and then strong commitment."

Drucker wrote (referring to the Ford Motor Company's disastrous Edsel project in 1958): "And so when it got into trouble, nobody supported the child. I'm not saying it could have been a success. But without that personal commitment it certainly never could be."[9]

5. Expect Positive Results

"There is a cautionary tale. One must not be a 'Pollyanna.' Still the central thought is correct. One cannot be negative and succeed in anything."

Drucker supported this "law of leadership" because of his strong belief that there were just two essentials for any business. One is marketing; the other, innovation. Innovation requires a change leader who has to expect positive results because going against old ways, especially when the business is successful, always means overcoming the opposition's tendency to declare, "If it ain't broke, don't fix it." Yet that's exactly when change must occur, according to Drucker.

6. Take Care of Your People

"Many managers are failing to do this, and it will catch up with them."

Drucker wrote: "A leader has responsibility to his subordinates, to his associates."[10]

7. Duty Before Self

This point requires some further definition. What I meant by this is that leaders have a duty to accomplish the mission and a duty to take care of those for whom they are responsible. Addressing a leader's own needs must come only after fulfilling this duty.

"This should be the basis of all leadership. The leader cannot act in personal interests. It must be in the interests of the customer and the worker. This is the great weakness of American management today."

Drucker wrote: "Douglas MacArthur . . . built a team second to none because he put the task first. . . . He was also unbelievably vain, with a tremendous contempt for humanity, because he was certain that no one came close to him in intelligence. Neverthe-less, he forced himself in every single staff conference to start the presentation with the most junior officer. He did not allow anybody to interrupt."[11]

8. Get Out in Front

"Very true—as junior leader or as CEO the leader must be where the work is the most challenging. During World War I losses among higher-ranking officers were rare compared with the losses they caused by their incompetence. Too few generals were killed."

Drucker wrote: "The human being himself determines what he contributes."[12]

Drucker on the Heart of Leadership

Drucker agreed with the principles of leadership I had uncovered. He spoke in strong support of each, but especially of the first—maintaining absolute integrity. However, he added that there were other useful principles of leadership, among them that a manager must first decide to be a leader. While all of the principles I had uncovered from battle leadership would help, the prime principle, according to Drucker, was what I called "duty before self." "A leader, any leader," he said, "must be for the benefit of others and not for oneself." In his writings, I discovered that it was this that he felt distinguished true leaders from "misleaders" such as Hitler and Stalin.

CHAPTER 15

Leadership for Upper Management

Some years ago I was in my office preparing for a lecture on leadership for a graduate course I was teaching at a nearby university when I received a call from the chair of the department of leadership at the Air War College in Montgomery, Alabama. Like the Industrial College of the Armed Forces and the National War College in other branches of the military, the Air War College has a unique mission. It is to take some of the best officers, with outstanding records and twenty or more years of service, and prepare them for top leadership positions in the U.S. military. Entrance to these schools is highly competitive, even though not all those who attend make it to the top ranks. Of the several thousand outstanding leaders in each service, only a handful can be promoted to general or admiral every year. This is reasonable and acceptable.

What was neither reasonable nor acceptable was that despite many years of proven performance and screening, many of those who were promoted simply failed in their performance as top military executives. This was costing the government a great deal of money. Worse, this occurred in peacetime; at war, the costs could be even greater in treasure, consequences, and human sacrifice.

The caller noted that Dr. Owen Jacobs at the Industrial College of the Armed Forces (ICAF) had developed a program to address this issue and they intended to develop a similar program at the Air War College. Although they had already been in contact with Dr. Jacobs, they wanted my input as a retired Air Force general and the author of several books on leadership. They felt that as a graduate of the ICAF, albeit before the arrival of Dr. Jacobs and the development of his program, I might have unique insight on this topic. Moreover they asked if I would be willing lecture on "strategic leadership," and to define why the problem of failure in the top ranks exists, and what the Air Force could do about it.

An Old Problem That Has Only Gotten Worse

Now, this is not a new problem in either the military or the civilian world. Leaders with records of outstanding performance have failed after reaching top positions throughout history. Drucker recognized this. "The most common cause of executive failure is inability or unwillingness to change with the demands of a new position. The executive who keeps on doing what he has done successfully before he moved is almost bound to fail."[1] Despite Peter's insight, little proactive work was done to reduce the failure rate. That a certain number failed was a given.

This problem has worsened significantly in both the military and business. In business, millions—if not billions—of dollars are lost every year to this issue. According to an article in the *National Post*, over a ten-year period, one-third of Fortune 500 chief executives lasted less than three years in the job. Estimates of overall CEO failure rates are as high as 75 percent, and rarely less than 30 percent. In a single ten-year period, CEO departures due to poor performance increased by 20 percent.[2] These rates are increasing. A 40 percent increase occurred in a single recent year, and the historical trend is far worse. A CEO hired in the 1990s was 300 percent more likely to be fired than one hired before 1980,[3] One venture capitalist, who had observed many new CEOs, said, "The failure rate of first time CEOs is incredibly high."[4] In the first nine months of 2008, 1,132 CEOs of well-established firms left their posts, and the pace for the year seemed likely to well exceed the previous record of 1,478 set in 2006.[5]

An added complication is that all leaders must learn early on to be strategic leaders, generally before becoming top executives. Because of technology, among other factors, a junior "tactical" executive can be in the same situation as a senior-level strategic leader. For example, middle managers may be required to lead multidiscipline teams outside their own specialties about which they may have little knowledge, and for which, like top executives, they are accountable.

The Leap from Tactical to Strategic

The time lines of the tactical leader have been short for some time, and are no longer confined to the tactical. Jimmy Doolittle raided Tokyo and other Japanese cities flying B-25 medium bombers off the aircraft carrier *Hornet* only four months after the Japanese attack on Pearl Harbor in the early days of World War II. The intent was to get within five hundred miles of the Japanese coast before launching these bombers. By stretching the bombers to their maximum range, the planes could land at bases in China, from which they could be recovered. However, the Japanese spotted the task force ten hours and almost two hundred miles from their intended launch position, which meant that the planes would not be able to reach the Chinese bases after the attack. Doolittle and Navy Captain Marc Mitscher had to make the decision to launch anyway or to call the attack off. They decided to launch. Although the planes hit their targets and none was shot down, because of this tactical decision every single aircraft ran out of fuel and crash-landed.

However, the consequences of this tactical decision were strategic in nature and were felt not only over the short term of days, weeks, or months, but also for much longer because, among other things, the Japanese were forced to withdraw significant numbers of aircraft back to Japan for home island defense. More important, the attack gave the United States confidence that it would ultimately win, while it did the opposite for Japan. Although Japan had not launched a failed offensive since fighting began in 1935, no major Japanese offensive succeeded after Doolittle's attack.

Thus, although the basics of leadership have not changed in thousands of years, modern technology has fueled major changes in the approach to strategy, which have had a major impact on leadership responsibilities and the outcomes of their decision making, especially at higher levels in the organization.

The failure of the tactical leader to breach the barrier between tactical and strategic often carries a heavy cost, both in increased waste and in opportunities lost, whether of lives and treasure in the military or of output and profit in civilian life. In the past, we have simply discarded those who could not make the transition to strategic leader and rewarded those that could. We bore the cost, and the failed individuals involved generally lost their careers, were shunted aside, or started new careers elsewhere. Neither nations nor companies nor organizations can afford this cost.

Performance attributes required of the strategic leader are more demanding than ever and the need for success continues to increase. Advancing technology requires complex operations that integrate many functional areas and require expertise in areas from which such leaders were once specifically excluded, including political, economic, and social issues.

For instance, if today's leaders don't understand how to lead a diverse workforce, not only can they suffer labor unrest, but also (if dealing with the government) may subject their organization to fines or punitive action. Perhaps even more important, such leaders aren't going to be able to take advantage of diversity while many competitors will, putting the organization at a definite competitive disadvantage. A company not led by strategic leaders who can capitalize on the strengths of those they lead may not even survive. In addition, the rise of the multinational corporation, joint ventures, international ownership, and even the Internet has provided problems and opportunities for top corporate leaders.

The Challenge of Specialization

Researchers into strategic management in the military found that leaders promoted to higher executive ranks must lead differently from the way they successfully led when they were "tactical leaders." At the same time, some very senior and very well-intentioned military executives still recommended that newly selected junior generals "not do anything different" from what they had previously done.[6] This is clearly a mistaken notion for military and nonmilitary leaders alike.

More than forty years ago, Drucker predicted the rise of "the knowledge worker," and, because of increasing technology, this phenomenon is growing. There is just too much to master. Therefore, many of the new executive's subordinates will have knowledge about and be able to do things in areas where the CEO has little expertise. Whereas once new top leaders could pride themselves on being able to do any job that a subordinate could do, this is usually no longer possible. This realization can be discomforting and present new challenges.

Drucker used a military example to illustrate the problem: "A regimental commander in the army, only a few decades ago, had held every one of the jobs of his subordinates—battalion commander, company commander, platoon commander. The only difference in these respective jobs between the lowly platoon commander and the lordly regimental commander was in the number of people each commands; the work was exactly alike."[7] Drucker explained that today's senior commanders not only perform many different jobs, with much less time in line executive jobs, but also many of the officers they lead do much different work, and they may never have commanded these types of subordinate units.

Today's top executives will increasingly work with different kinds of people from a host of companies with different ideas and different cultures, speaking different languages, who have different ways of operating. Forty years ago, less than 7 percent of U.S. corporations were involved in foreign trade or joint ventures. Today, again due to expanding technology, these percentages are for the most part reversed. Even a one-person company may engage in business internationally.

Technology demands specialization. A corporation cannot maintain its competitive position by retaining highly trained specialists who may only be needed infrequently. It is much more efficient to subcontract, joint venture, or hire external specialists when needed. Even the U.S. military, which once was almost entirely self-sufficient, today frequently contracts for everything from meal service to security outside "the company." In addition, communication, bolstered once again by technology, requires that leaders at increasingly lower levels in the organization deal with the media, senior members of other organizations, and more. These factors help explain why the failure rate among senior executives, and maybe all executives, is growing.

The Responsibility of the Organization for Selection

Drucker believed that proven executive talent was too valuable to waste in "human sacrifice." This is one reason why he so strongly opposed "The Peter Principle," mentioned in earlier chapters, which said that every manager rose to his or her level of incompetence. Such managers, stated Professor Laurence Peter, must then be discharged lest eventually all of top management be peopled by incompetents, which would invariably cause the organization to fail.[8]

Drucker agreed that an organization should not tolerate incompetence. However, in his view, the failure of a subordinate executive was usually caused more by the executive who appointed the person to the position than by the individual elevated. When he made these comments, Drucker was focused on selection and appointment for an identified position (see Chapter Thirteen), not promotion in general to senior executive levels from middle or upper middle management. Thus, reducing failure rates through better selection procedures is only part of the solution. The other part is that future higher-level leaders must assume significant responsibility for readying and preparing themselves for this higher level of leadership, with its broadened responsibilities and complexities.

How to Prepare for High-Level Leadership

Drucker never directly addressed what the individual could and should do to prepare for top-level leadership. However, he did write extensively on the individual's personal development and left many clues from his own life. From these, I have distilled four Drucker prescriptions:

- Manage your own preparation for top management.
- Master a discipline outside your profession.
- Read extensively in and outside your primary specialty.
- Think, discuss, and write.

Manage Your Own Preparation for Top Management

While Peter did not ignore management's responsibility for selection and promotion, he knew that ultimately it was future top executives who had to ensure their readiness to perform once selected. In the introduction to *Management Challenges for the Twenty-First Century*, he devoted a chapter to this subject. In it, he pointed out:

"The very great achievers, a Napoleon, a Leonardo da Vinci, a Mozart, have always managed themselves. This in large measure made them great achievers, but they were the rarest of exceptions. And they were so unusual, both in their talents and in their achievements, as to be considered outside the boundaries of normal human existence."[9]

Drucker noted that, in today's environment, a knowledge worker might not have the endowments of these examples, but all must accept the responsibility to manage themselves. Most large organizations have management development programs, spaced throughout an employee's career to help develop potential senior leaders. Drucker was aware of them. However, the people the corporation chose to participate in these programs tended to be those already selected for advancement regardless of the level at which the program was initiated. Drucker recommended that leaders not rely on or wait to attend these programs, and stressed that leaders themselves had to prepare for higher-level responsibilities.

Master a Separate Discipline Outside Your Profession

In class, Drucker told a story, probably allegorical, of a CEO who died suddenly. At his funeral, business associates were amazed to see a group of Egyptologists among the mourners, and vice versa. It seemed that in addition to being a well-liked CEO, the man was a world-famous Egyptologist. Neither group knew of the man's other profession.

Drucker's point was that leaders needed to develop their expertise in an entirely different field. He saw several advantages:

- Leaders would develop self-confidence in their ability to succeed in an entirely different field. The military challenges leaders to do this almost automatically by varying assignments throughout a career.

- Acquiring expertise simultaneously also offers a mental break from the pressures of concentrating on a single profession.

- The biggest breakthroughs frequently come not from inside a profession, but by applying something true in one profession but unknown in another.

Peter followed his own advice by becoming so expert in Japanese art that he held a professorship, taught, and coauthored a book on the subject.

Read Extensively In and Outside Your Primary Specialty

Some executives used to brag that they had not read a single book since leaving college. The time for such an approach is long past. The developments in any industry require extensive reading, even study, to keep up with them. General Ronald Fogleman, then chief of staff of the Air Force, mandated that on promotion to captain, young officers were to receive a selection of books on military topics as a gift of the Air Force. The idea was to encourage these young officers to read. This is something that might be profitably encouraged in all organizations on topics appropriate to their work.

Drucker himself employed this technique. His father wanted him to attend college immediately after completing what we call high school. Instead, he went to Hamburg and secured a business apprenticeship. However, at the same time, he attended law school at night and began a program of extensive reading beyond law, even including works of fiction, which lasted a lifetime.

Think, Discuss, and Write

Almost all leaders think about and discuss issues of interest, but few do this in a systematic way. Drucker learned to do this from his parents, who conducted weekly dinners that included many intellectuals; Peter, although still a teenager, was invited to participate. He continued this practice when I was his student, and it was clear he enjoyed the interchange and was disappointed when those present were reluctant or unable to engage in the discussion. He was capable of discussing almost any subject with lively interest.

Drucker saw writing as another way to prepare and broaden yourself for top-level management. Writing down ideas helps you develop the ideas and gain a better understand the subject. It is sometimes assumed that those who build successful careers on their ability to write have an innate ability to write, yet most writers claim that writing is a skill that can only be developed over time and with practice.

Drucker began writing and was actually published shortly after gaining his law degree. He also published a piece for a prestigious economic journal in 1929—in which he predicted that the bull market would continue for another ten years. That was just a month before the crash that led to the Great Depression. It was one of his few erroneous predictions. This did not deter him from writing; over his career, Drucker wrote on a variety of subjects including economics, politics, travel, and more, including two works of fiction.[10]

Drucker on Preparing for Top Management

Drucker believed the failure rate of top executive leaders was increasingly excessive and wasteful, but that it could be reduced substantially by more careful selection and by the individual leader's acceptance of responsibility for self-development and preparation before promotion. This could be accomplished by accepting responsibility for and managing one's own preparation for top management, mastering a separate discipline outside a primary profession, reading extensively in all fields, and thinking, discussing, and writing about topics of interest and importance.

PART FOUR

Motivation and Leadership

For years, even though Drucker almost completely ignored the topic of leadership as such, he wrote extensively about motivation. In his very first book, published in 1939, Drucker argued that in effect what dictatorships did was substitute security, stability, and order as a motivator for the traditional financial motivations provided by the capitalist system.[1]

Although he continued thinking and writing about motivation over the years, he did not make a connection between motivation and leadership, probably because he did not attempt to unify his theories of leadership until relatively late in his career. Yet Drucker did list *motivating* as one of the "basic operations" of a manager's work.[2]

Typically, his insights were bold, fearless, and explicit. At a time when permissive management was supposed to be the new direction of motivation, replacing so-called command-and-control leadership, Drucker took a different tack. While supporting the idea of self-direction and responsibility, he said this could not be accomplished without authority, guidance, and direction, that a leader must always be in charge, and that while "Theory X" no longer worked to achieve optimal performance in an organization, "Theory Y" without restraint was possibly worse.

Moreover, he claimed that "employee satisfaction" would lead to mediocrity at best and stated that what was really needed as a motivator was employee dissatisfaction. Although he felt that financial motivation by itself was a huge mistake, he believed altruism as the main motivator was inherently incorrect. And in one of his last warnings to managers of the new twenty-first century, he cautioned that in the future workers must be treated not simply as employees but also as volunteers. His advice to leaders on how leaders should motivate is unique, logical, and powerful.

CHAPTER 16

Leadership Style as a Motivator

New styles of leadership and their effects on motivation are a constant topic of discussion. Some term the most common style to be in vogue over the last fifty years "permissive leadership," which, in turn, is related to dozens of leadership concepts and techniques. "Permissive leadership" grew out of our experiences during World War II. With a U.S. military that had expanded over 1000 percent to include more than 13 percent of the population, with 16 million servicemen and women under arms, the military needed large numbers of new leaders fast. Therefore, they screened millions of people as best they could and selected those who tested best and trained them for leadership as rapidly as possible.

New officers were referred to as "ninety-day wonders" because there simply wasn't enough time to give them more training. Before the war, officer training took a minimum of six months and could require more than four years. But ninety days was all the time the tens of thousands of these new leaders could be spared. In many cases, these quickly trained leaders performed brilliantly. Unfortunately, a significant number did not. Some simply fell back on their legal authority to give orders and, by law, to have these orders enforced.

Simply giving orders is not leadership, and, after the war, the military recognized the need to revamp leadership training. Accordingly, the military encouraged, initiated, and funded a great deal of leadership research at universities around the country. Researchers began by studying leadership traits and went on from there. One of the more successful ideas that emerged led to a more flexible style of leadership whereby the leader delegated more aspects of the job to those led. Delegation was not new. In ancient times, leaders were admonished to tell their followers what to do but not how to do it. Even General Patton, a leader with a dominant style, taught: "Don't tell people how to do things. Tell them what to do and let them surprise you with their results."[1] However, the new emphasis encouraged more freedom for subordinate action and thinking and more openness on the part of the leader. One of the most widely read and adopted examples of the new open style was Douglas McGregor's concept of Theory X and Theory Y.[2]

Theory X and Theory Y

Douglas McGregor was a professor at the MIT Sloan School of Management. Although he did no research himself, he closely studied the work of others, including three of Drucker's books: *Concept of the Corporation*, *The New Society*, and *The Practice of Management*.[3] McGregor concluded that managers led by one of only two general theories of motivation. Leaders following Theory X (which closely resembled the carrot-and-stick approach) assumed that employees primarily work for money or when threatened with punishment and will avoid work if possible. They have little interest in the job or assuming responsibility for the outcome of their work. As a result, such employees must be closely supervised and controlled, using incentives to reward those who perform adequately and punishment for those who do not.

Theory Y leaders' assumptions and style of leadership were quite different. They assumed that employees were ambitious, self-motivated, and eager to accept greater responsibility for work outcome, if only encouraged and allowed to do so. They could lead themselves better if only permitted more authority over what they did and how it was done. Tight control and supervision was not the way to motivate them. In fact, it was counterproductive. Instead, a Theory Y leader let workers exercise self-control with as much self-direction and autonomy possible. In effect, the leader's permissive style empowered followers to do their best.

Drucker's Views on Theory X

Drucker agreed that Theory X was not the final answer, and, citing Xenophon's writings about Cyrus the Great's father, who recommended something like Theory Y, said this was known since antiquity.

However, there was more to it. With the rise of the knowledge worker, the number of jobs in which workers were expected to simply follow orders was continually declining. It's not so long ago that all employees were exhorted not to think but to do as they were told. A sign posted at the entrance to a large factory read, "Check your brain outside before entering." This was a clear warning not to think, and to just follow orders. However, the time for this approach was long past even when Drucker stated this fact more than thirty years ago.

Drucker's "knowledge workers," equipped with brainpower and a constantly expanding universe of intellectual and experiential resources, were increasingly needed for the organization to be competitive. In addition, knowledge workers knew their worth and the potential contribution of their ideas and expected to be consulted about their work. This in itself became a potential motivator, but also a potential de-motivator if knowledge workers and their ideas and inputs were arbitrarily ignored or excluded. Drucker concluded that the carrot-and-stick approach no longer worked for knowledge workers and, in developed countries, it didn't work for manual workers either.[4]

Drucker found fault with Theory X even when he admitted that, on occasion, it had worked. In speaking of compensation and benefits as a primary motivator, he said in class, "The problem with the carrot-and-stick approach is not that it hasn't worked, but that it has worked too well. This caused increasing demands for more and more until the limit was reached and the corporation was no longer competitive."

Problems with Theory Y

Yet Drucker did not accept permissive leadership in its entirety. He took strong exception to certain aspects of Theory Y, and what Drucker termed a laissez-faire style of leadership. According to Drucker, the biggest problem with Theory Y was not what McGregor had written, but how others had interpreted and applied it. Drucker said that McGregor did not intend Theory Y to mean permissiveness. It did not mean freedom from restraint, and, by itself, it was inadequate because by making the worker responsible and oriented toward achievement, it made impossibly high demands on both worker and leader.[5]

These demands were far from insignificant. Drucker credited Abraham Maslow, developer of the famous "hierarchy of needs," for pointing out that the demand for responsibility and achievement under Theory Y went beyond what any but the "strong and healthy" could fulfill. Maslow went so far as to call Theory Y "inhumane." Drucker concluded that a leader could not simply replace Theory X with Theory Y. Rather, the leader must replace the security and certainty provided by Theory X and provide by different means what commands and penalties once accomplished.[6]

Drucker had another major criticism of permissive leadership, which he repeated in many of his writings: "Knowledge workers still need a superior. The organizational structure must clearly identify where final decisions and ultimate responsibility rest."[7] In other words, the call for permissiveness did not mean the demise of the organizational leader or relegating the leader to some sort of figurehead status, a cheerleader, or a simple connection to more senior executives. On the contrary, the Theory Y leader's job was much more difficult than the Theory X leader's because the responsibilities of leadership under Theory Y were significantly greater than they had been under Theory X.

The Responsibilities of Theory Y Leaders

"One does not manage people," Drucker insisted. "One must lead them." True leadership was far more than giving orders, rewarding those who carried them out efficiently and effectively, and punishing those who did not.

What were the added responsibilities under Theory Y? For many types of knowledge work, productivity was, and is, not easy to define and therefore not easy to measure. You can't do it by calculating the ability to carry out orders. That's Theory X. Yet measurement is necessary, for example, to know whether your team is moving forward. The goal is no longer obedience—it is achievement. There's a difference. You don't simply want workers to put in time, you want them to be highly productive and to achieve the objective. Doing this depends as much on the workers' ability, intellect, and work as on your own as leader.

Drucker, using the example of a salesperson, explained the difficulty of measuring productivity under Theory Y. Do you measure the salesperson's productivity by total sales, by profitability, by the ability to bring in new customers, service accounts, introduce new products, by some relationship with territory, or what? Earlier I used sales to demonstrate an output that is easily measured, but, as Drucker's analysis makes clear, even that is not so simple.

Also, should such things as dependability and reliability be factored in? The sales manager or other higher-level manager can and does calculate incentives and set priorities. However, simply measuring productivity quantitatively is not sufficient because of the number of factors. It's a moving target, and much of the responsibility for implementing general guidelines and deciding what to do must be delegated to the individual on the firing line, the salesperson.[8] This is true for thousands of types of work performed by knowledge workers. Being a Theory Y manager and worker is hard work!

That's not all. Theory Y workers need a challenge, and they need to know how everything fits together. They need to know the organization's mission and to be convinced that it is worthwhile. They need to see the results of their work and to know how they are doing. They want to know the facts. The leader must also recognize that not all followers can be led and motivated in the same way. Each needs to be led differently, and led differently at different times. Only in this way can Theory Y followers and leaders function to make the theory work (and it is not clear that all can) so that the worker shares responsibility and, together with the leader, can achieve the goal.

When Theory X Leadership Is Acceptable

Peter did not address this question directly, but he came close to implying that there are times when elements of Theory X are appropriate, even for a Theory Y leader. Psychologists tell us that individuals are motivated *toward* pleasure or *away from* pain. A single individual's perception may vary in different situations or environments. However, in general a person's preferred tendency falls into one of these two categories. Some workers will not be as motivated by the responsibility and possibilities inherent in Theory Y, but are motivated by avoiding the punishment or pain associated with failing to achieve what the leader desires. For such workers, benefits or rewards offered under either Theory X or Theory Y may have minimal effect as a motivational tool, but the "stick" may be a necessary tool under both theories, as is the "carrot" in reverse circumstances.

Five Dimensions of Work

Drucker described five dimensions of working: physiological, psychological, social, economic, and power. All are separate and need to be analyzed independently. However, as motivators they operate together in any work situation. Moreover and unfortunately, their demands are very different and frequently pull in different, if not opposite, directions. Yet they not only are present at the same time, they also must be managed simultaneously.

The traditional approach to management, leadership, and motivation is to treat one of these, depending on whose concept you follow, as the dominant dimension.[9] Therefore, you have advocates recommending motivational systems and models based on economics, social equality and diversity, Japanese management, Total Quality Management (TQM), reengineering, knowledge management (KM), Drucker's own management by objectives (MBO), Theory Y, shared management, and more. Drucker labeled this the "fallacy of the dominant dimension."

There is no question but that the research, analysis, and application of these various concepts add to the leader's understanding and knowledge of leadership and ability to motivate workers to achieve. The problem is that each one claims to be the dominant theory, the one a leader and the organization needs to follow to ensure ultimate and continual success. These and other ideas led to what *Fortune* magazine called "Management by Fad."

Building on Drucker's "fallacy of the dominant dimension" one can see great danger in viewing these ideas as be-alls and end-alls to leadership and management. Some organizations that adopted TQM went so far as to declare that if any individual failed to go along and adopt the TQM philosophy, the organization's whole TQM system would not work. Maverick "nonbelievers" had to be educated, persuaded, threatened with punishment, or dismissed from the organization!

While Drucker saw Theory Y as the more correct general approach for motivation, compared to Theory X, he did not view it or any other management philosophy—even MBO, his own management system—as the only one.[10] Many if not most of the techniques embedded in these concepts would work and add value, if done right. However, it was the leader's application of these elements that was crucial to their success. Although he believed in Theory Y, he said that it was foolish to deny that financial reward was not a motivation. People were just not universally altruistic. Thus it was up to the leader to lead correctly under Theory Y.

How to Make Theory Y Work

Drucker agreed that leaders must recognize that knowledge workers usually don't produce their best when fear is the motivator. Therefore, if your style has been carrot-and-stick, better take the advice of Cyrus the Great's father and think again. However, Drucker believed in several essentials. Foremost, that Theory Y didn't mean unrestrained laissez-faire leadership. If anything, the leader must be even more involved than the Theory X leader.

Next, leaders must remember that the goal of Theory Y is to get each worker to continually *achieve* a personal best working synergistically with others, which is accomplished by emphasizing performance, not obedience. It's fine to adopt various concepts and to apply them through education and motivational policies. That's smart leadership and can help leaders understand leadership and expand their own ideas.

Leaders should not make a religion out of any one concept. No matter what advocates claim, none is the dominant dimension for leading, and all dimensions—physiological, psychological, social, economic, and power—must be recognized, considered, and managed simultaneously by the leader. Adopting a philosophy emphasizing one dimension means management by fad, and no matter how good the idea, no fad lasts forever. Leadership does.

Drucker on Style and Motivation

Leading people under Theory Y is much more difficult than during the carrot-and-stick days of Theory X. You are still the leader, with full responsibility for getting the job done. You cannot abrogate this. At times, your role may be "benevolent dictator"; at other times, much leadership work will be assumed by those you lead, a form of shared leadership. Throughout, each worker must be treated differently, and there are times that each must be treated differently from that worker's norm. Without this, the organization will never achieve the maximum productivity sought. Even with the most participative form of Theory Y, you can delegate authority, but you can never delegate overall responsibility. Overall responsibility for everything an organization or anyone in it accomplishes, or fails to accomplish, belongs to the organization's leader, just as it did in the time of Xenophon and Cyrus the Great.

CHAPTER 17

Motivating to Peak Performance

Drucker emphasized that Theory Y, or any permissive, open, or worker-shared leadership style, necessitated additional responsibilities and effort for both leader and worker for two main reasons. First, the emphasis was no longer on obedience to the leader but on performance, and achieving performance was far more complex. As a corollary, the worker was expected to contribute significantly to the goal set by the leader.

The word *performance* does not adequately describe what Drucker had in mind. The considerable additional effort on the part of both leader and worker must lead to positive results, or the investment, risk, and effort involved is inefficient and wasteful—and Theory X would probably obtain better results. Mere performance therefore is insufficient.

The goal and outcome must be *outstanding performance*, achieved, of course, through worker responsibility. The difference between performance and outstanding performance is the difference between participating in an athletic sport and winning an Olympic Gold Medal, between grilling a hamburger and creating a five-star entrée, between acting in a home video and winning an Oscar. In addition, outstanding performance can motivate, which makes it even more important. Therefore, we must seek peak performance.

The question then is how leaders motivate workers to achieve peak performance. Drucker said a leader must create "a responsible worker," and suggested four ways to accomplish this task. Before I list them, though, it's useful to look at a method that sounds good, and is attempted by many organizations, but does not work.

Employee Satisfaction Will Not Motivate Performance

Eventually almost every organization conducts surveys to determine "employee satisfaction." Once initiated, these surveys reappear from time to time and probably always will. These surveys do have some uses. They present an opportunity for employees to vent about irritants. They give leaders a feel for the major issues of concern in their organizations at that particular time. They may provide guidance for management decisions. However, as Drucker noted, they have significant limitations.

"Employee satisfaction" is not easily defined and cannot be usefully quantified. For example, one cannot say that employees are satisfied, even if 75 percent of workers agree with "This is a good place to work." I have worked in organizations where satisfaction/ dissatisfaction studies were completely misused and worded to elicit desired responses to various planned or desired courses of action.

Drucker's biggest criticism was simply that "satisfaction" or "dissatisfaction" responses were inadequate and did not result in a responsible worker. Nor could a leader buy responsibility with financial rewards. Thus satisfaction alone could not have a positive impact on creating responsibility and therefore on performance, and satisfaction by itself certainly cannot motivate peak performance.[1] In fact, Drucker wrote that a worker's dissatisfaction with some aspect of the work was far more likely to do that, if it stimu-lated action to improve the situation and the worker was empow-ered to take that action.

Drucker's Four Paths to Creating the Responsible Worker

If satisfaction isn't the key for creating the responsible worker, what is? Drucker found four paths: placing workers carefully, demanding high standards of performance, providing the worker with needed information, and encouraging a managerial vision. These aren't alternative approaches; all four must be used to achieve the desired results.

Placing Workers Carefully

I discussed Drucker's concepts about staffing in Chapter Thirteen. Drucker's strong feeling about this aspect of leadership cannot be underestimated. In one class in which we discussed staffing and the selection of senior executives, Peter gave us a case to write up and later discuss concerning a failed senior promotion.

In addition to the obvious problem of putting the wrong person in the job, Drucker taught that a systematic, serious, and continual effort to put people in the right jobs was a prerequisite to high motivation.

Here we come up against a conflict between two of Drucker's ideas. As discussed, Drucker admired the military model of lead-ership. However, one aspect of promotion in the military, also employed by many civilian organizations, is placing people in vari-ous positions to gain experience in other areas and to test their ability to adapt outside of their comfort zone. Drucker seemed to applaud this concept as a way to master high executive leadership. The other is his belief in careful placement for success.

How then do the two ideas fit together? Drucker found no problem with the idea of varied assignments for an executive to

Who's at Fault?

The executive promoted, a man given the name "Novak," had a fine record of increasing responsibility over many years with the company. The CEO, called "McQuinn," had no doubt that Novak was the right man for the job, and he made the appointment without consultation, and without thinking through the job requirements completely. For the first time in his career, Novak failed miserably in his new position. McQuinn, shocked, decided that Novak had no excuse and the appropriate solution was to fire him. However, the chairman had a policy that all senior firings had to be discussed first with him first. McQuinn met with the chairman.

The chairman asked McQuinn what had happened. McQuinn told him that Novak made serious errors in judgment, which had cost the company a great deal of money. Pressed further, McQuinn could not offer much other than that the job was too much for Novak and that he had gone as far up the corporate ladder as he could.

Much to McQuinn's surprise, the chairman blamed him for Novak's failure, saying, "The one thing we know for certain is that you made a mistake, since Novak was your appointment." To fire Novak, he said, was unfair, and it was stupid. "Why should we lose a proven manager as valuable as Novak, just because you made a mistake?"[2]

gain experience or to be tested. However, in the case "Who's at Fault?" McQuinn did not make the appointment in question for this purpose. Had he done so, Novak would have been expected to make some mistakes. However, since McQuinn did not make the appointment for these objectives, Drucker viewed this as a type of assignment requiring careful placement. In reality, there was no contradiction in Drucker's position regarding this issue.

Demanding High Standards of Performance

Adequate performance is associated with easy, low-demand work. For peak performance, workers need much more. Essentially this means work that engages and challenges their abilities and motivates them with high standards. The idea that placing easier demands de-motivates workers and placing heavier demands motivates them seems counterintuitive, but it is how things work. In my life in the military I observed that many highly competent people purposely avoided easy, mundane work and instead sought and volunteered for difficult, challenging, and even dangerous jobs.

I first learned this as a motivational concept from a University of Chicago professor, Thomas Whistler, when I was studying for my MBA. Whistler used one of his most brilliant and capable former doctoral students as an example. This student's first job after receiving his doctorate was at a major corporation, but in a relatively low position. This gifted student had apparently failed to perform to expectations and feeling this himself, had resigned, and joined another corporation where he had immediately done so well that within six months he had been elevated to the position of vice president. Professor Whistler invited us to speculate about the reason for this surprising personal turnaround.

Our ideas ranged from a personality conflict between the student's initial superior to personal problems outside of work to the job being beyond the capabilities of a new graduate, even one with a Ph.D. None was correct. "The problem," Whistler said, "was not that the job was too big, but that the job was too small. The only mistake my former student made was to accept that job in the first place. My student had this amount of ability (Whistler raised his hand far above his head) and that first job required this amount (Whistler lowed his hand to about his knee)." In a sense, this was the opposite of the Peter Principle, discussed in earlier chapters.

I had never heard anything like this previously. I had always been taught that there were no small jobs, only small people. Over the years since, I have seen many individuals like this one who did a poor or mediocre job when unchallenged, but rose to accomplish the most difficult, seemingly impossible, tasks when properly challenged.

Charles Garfield, a psychologist with degrees in both psychology and mathematics, found this particularly true of what he called "peak performance individuals." In working with NASA during the first launch of astronauts to the moon, Garfield was amazed to discover that many individuals who previously had done only mediocre work had suddenly "caught fire" and were doing things that neither they nor anyone else had even thought possible. However, immediately after the moon landings had been accomplished, they fell back to earth and performed only adequately. They and their superiors treated the whole peak performance experience as an aberration.[3] Too bad. Properly led, they could have continued doing the impossible far into the future.

Some years ago, I heard about a nonunion company called Oberg Industries, a tool and die company. Oberg Industries was located right in the middle of union country in Western Pennsylvania. You might think that its nonunion status was due to easy working conditions with few demands. Not so. Oberg had a fifty-hour work week with only a fifteen-minute break for lunch allowed for both management and labor. Don Oberg, the founder and then president, was no easy touch. *Inc.* magazine called him "The Lord of Discipline."[4] Yet despite the founder's deserved title, potential employees lined up to work there. At the time, annual sales for most tool-and-die companies were on average $2 million a year. At Oberg, sales were $27 million, and sales per employee were, on average, 30 percent higher than in other tool-and-die companies. There was no recession that year, yet sixteen hundred people applied for only thirty job openings.

Of course Oberg employees were well paid. However, far more important than compensation, Don Oberg, while a hard taskmaster, had managed to convince his employees that if you met Oberg's difficult challenges, you were the best. This exemplifies the fact that being a Theory Y leader does not mean that you are a soft touch and needn't make demands on those led. By the way, Oberg Industries logs over $125 million in sales annually today.[5]

However, Drucker knew one important point about setting high standards that many do not—and that others completely ignore. High standards are not for the worker alone. Leaders must set and enforce high standards for themselves as well.[6] In other words, you must set the example, get out in front, and allow your high standards to motivate to peak performance. I have seen corporate executives make rousing speeches about how important a particular action is, exhorting their followers to keep at it until the job gets done, and then wave good-bye and head off to play golf. That's not demanding the high standards Drucker spoke about and is not leadership.

Providing the Worker with Information Needed

It is essential that workers be given the information they need—whether they ask for it or not—to help them reach peak performance. Drucker didn't touch on this, but if a worker isn't enthusiastic about acquiring information that the leader feels is necessary, it is the leader's responsibility to explain its importance. Only with information can workers control, measure, and guide themselves to reaching the goal and accepting complete responsibility for it.

Moreover, as Drucker explained, it is critical that workers know and understand how what they do contributes to the work of the entire organization, and, after that, how the organization's work contributes to society. Such information about the big picture helps in acquiring managerial vision, the last of the four ways Drucker identified to motivate workers to responsibility and peak performance.[7]

Encouraging Managerial Vision

Drucker's main reason for encouraging managerial vision had to do with workers' seeing their work as contributing to the survival or success of the enterprise. Only in this way can workers feel the pride necessary for peak performance.[8]

Other important things motivate this same pride. Workers motivated to peak performance must be able to operate without oversight, or even the possibility of referring to a higher authority when the boss is gone. Without managerial vision, it is impossible for workers to operate independently at the level needed to avoid suboptimization at the expense of the whole. Moreover, operating at peak performance frequently requires risk, which takes self-confidence. This means that the knowledge worker's self-confidence is essential, and the leader must play a part in its development because you cannot give someone either pride or accomplishment.[9] Finally, taking a leaf from the military model, Drucker recognized that to have true responsibility, knowledge workers—at whatever level—must be able to lead.

To develop knowledge workers as leaders requires leadership experience.[10] Therefore, leaders must play an active role in developing leadership in their subordinates by providing leadership opportunities in the plant community and encouraging the workers to step up to accept them. Drucker gave some examples—running Red Cross blood drives, Christmas parties, and employee publications—but the possibilities are practically unlimited.

I call these "uncrowned" leadership positions, since they do not usually involve permanent appointments or formal authority over others. Yet they are wonderful for building self-confidence and gaining leadership experience, and of course providing the pride and motivation to the peak performance that you are looking for. For the individual knowledge worker, they may be more important in career development than regularly assigned duties. One of the most rapid career advancements I ever saw in industry was of a young engineer given the unwanted task of bond salesman. He did so well in this short-term, non-engineering job that it led in quick succession to responsibility for engineering jobs and eventually to a very early promotion to vice president.

Drucker on Motivation

Drucker didn't doubt that, correctly done, a Theory Y style could be a motivator. But as noted, Drucker believed that this requires much of both leader and follower. It's certainly not a case of simply identifying what employees are happy or unhappy about; it requires real leadership on the part of the leader, which means simultaneously paying attention to who is assigned to what position, demanding high levels of performance, providing the workers with necessary information, and encouraging managerial vision.

CHAPTER 18

Charisma as a Motivator

harisma motivates. Look at the 2008 election. Obama's charisma first propelled him to his party's candidacy over Hillary Clinton, who was considered a shoo-in, despite the fact that Obama was a one-term senator and had limited national experience, and despite Clinton's senatorial experience, name recognition, and contacts. One formerly doubtful television reporter came away from one of Obama's early campaign rallies and gushed on national TV, "I've been Obamaized!" The same charisma overwhelmed the much-respected but less charismatic John McCain, and helped Obama claim nine million newly registered Democratic voters who ultimately helped him win the election.[1]

Perhaps because of his experience with Nazism in Europe, Drucker did not acknowledge charisma as a quality a leader could or should develop, in fact he pointed to successful leaders who lacked charisma, although not everyone agreed with his assessment. Drucker contrasted General George Marshall and President Truman with John F. Kennedy, who, he said, may have been the most charismatic person ever to occupy the White House. "Yet," he went on, "few presidents got as little done."[2]

Probably the only president to rival Kennedy for charisma in modern times was Ronald Reagan. However, in one of Peter's last interviews, he spoke first about Truman and his effectiveness, and then said, "The other effective president of the last 100 years was Ronald Reagan. His great strength was not charisma, as is commonly thought, but that he knew exactly what he could do and what he could not do."[3]

Even at this late stage of his life, Drucker was not a fan of charisma, despite its known power to motivate. He wrote, "Indeed, charisma becomes the undoing of leaders. It makes them inflexible, convinced of their own infallibility, unable to change."[4] Yet in writing about what effective managers should do, Drucker provided a description that closely parallels many of the actions of charismatic leaders.

Drucker was well aware that research counted charisma an important part of transformational leadership. Transformational leadership is based on aspirations of leader and follower, as opposed to transactional leadership, which is based on authority, and a form of Theory X.

Was Drucker Right?

If Drucker is taken at his word, all leaders should avoid charisma like the plague, and maybe even worry a little if anyone compliments them on being charismatic. Certainly Drucker was right in believing that some very effective leaders are in no way "charismatic," and that some charismatic leaders leave much to be desired when it comes to either ethics or performance. Nonetheless, Drucker recommended aspects of charisma without connecting them directly to that particular quality. In this chapter, I focus on those aspects of charisma that Drucker, without using the term, recommended to leaders.

Charisma Defined

The ancient Greeks defined charisma as a gift from the gods. Modern definitions allude to a personal leadership quality involving personal magnetism that permits leaders to arouse fervent popular devotion and enthusiasm. Both qualities tend to motivate workers toward high performance.

Charisma can influence and arouse enthusiasm in others. In one study involving more than two hundred subjects in a competition to identify future scientists, British professor Richard Wiseman found that competitors who scored highest in their ability to convey their emotions to others also progressed furthest in the competition, independent of prior accomplishments or the extent of their education.[5] As it turns out, the ability to convey emotions is an important component of charisma.

For several years, I was on the Academic Advisory Board of Vector Marketing, Inc., which sells high-quality cutlery under the brand name Cutco. One of the company's divisions, K-bar, made the original and world-famous Marine Corps k-bar knife during World War II. Most of Vector's sales force consists of students working part time.

A charismatic young student, Zach Lutsky, put himself through college as a Vector salesperson. Lutsky wanted to go to medical school after graduation. Unfortunately, outside work and good grades do not always go together, and his school counselor told him that he didn't have sufficiently high grades. Zach applied anyway. After being rejected by the medical school of his choice, he called the dean to ask if he could fly to Chicago from California for a face-to-face interview. The dean reluctantly granted the interview, stating tactfully that she didn't think he would be able to enter medical school with his grades—there were just so many openings, and it was just too competitive. Zach convinced the dean to meet with him anyway.

During the interview, Zach explained that he had to work to put himself through college, and showed the dean his sales record. The dean was impressed, probably, as in the future scientist study, as much with Zach's charisma as with his accomplishments. Of course, there were no openings. The dean advised him to prepare himself further and to apply again the following year, although she still held out little hope. Zach returned to his home town in Thousand Oaks, California, and made plans to follow the dean's advice. He was going to try again the following year. However, three days before medical school was to begin, he received a telegram from the dean's office. At the last minute, a previously accepted student had canceled. Zach was told that if he could be there in three days, the spot was his. Charisma, combined with hard work, the right attitude, and a lot of luck can have an impact on influencing and motivating no matter how hopeless the situation might look.

The ancient view was that someone was either born with charisma or not. The modern view is quite different. There is considerable evidence that charisma is not something one is born with, although certainly one might have a predisposition to acquiring it. Ronald Riggio, an academic researcher, discovered that "charisma is not something given to a person. It is not an inherited or inborn quality. Charisma is something that develops over time." Therefore, every leader could develop charisma. It is not a single characteristic or trait but an array of specific and powerful social skills employed either consciously or unconsciously by those considered by others to possess this quality.[6]

To show that charisma can be acquired, Riggio uses the example of none other than John Kennedy. As a young man, Kennedy and his friend Charles Spaulding visited Hollywood. Spaulding reported that Kennedy was so fascinated by the charisma displayed by the Hollywood stars they met that he became almost obsessed with their magnetism and strongly desired to acquire this quality.[7] Kennedy intentionally set out to become more charismatic by observing and practicing the actions of the Hollywood actors he met and observed.

Are Charismatic Leaders "Misleaders"?

Some charismatic leaders clearly are "misleaders," as Drucker maintained. Others follow these individuals only to learn of their folly when it is too late. Hitler and Stalin are probably the best-known examples of misleaders in the last century, although others could be named in every field of endeavor. Even if the charismatic leader is not intrinsically evil, there can be problems.

Contrariwise, far more charismatic leaders take their organizations and followers down the right path. Many researchers agree that charisma can be extremely powerful in leading others not only to achieve successful results but also sometimes to accomplish the highly unlikely and nearly impossible. How else might one explain the successes of college dropouts Steve Jobs, Bill Gates, and Steven Spielberg? Not that being a college dropout is required. The same might be said of the leadership of scientist Andy Grove at Intel, or lawyer Herb Kelleher at Southwest Airlines. History demonstrates that charisma can be an extremely positive motivational factor that should not be ignored.

Researching and Developing Charisma

Charisma researchers and writers generally approach the topic in one of three ways:

- They conduct experiments or observe the actions of charismatic and noncharismatic individuals to discover how charisma is applied.

- They conduct experiments or observe the actions of charismatic and noncharismatic individuals to discover the components of charisma.

- They conduct historical research, sometimes combined with observation of charismatic individuals in various settings, to determine what charismatics do.

Professor Wiseman, who led the study of new scientists, is a good example of the first approach. His research led him to recommend the following steps to those who would become more charismatic:

1. Maintain an open body posture with hands away from face when talking. Stand straight, but relaxed, hands apart and with palms forward or upward.

2. When dealing with individuals, let them know that they matter and that you enjoy being around them. Develop a genuine smile and nod when others talk, even briefly touching them on the upper arm. Maintain eye contact throughout.

3. When relating to a group, act comfortable in your leadership. Move around to appear enthusiastic while leaning slightly forward and looking at all parts of the group.

4. In your message, move beyond the status quo and strive to make a difference, being controversial, new, easy to understand, and counterintuitive.

5. In speaking, be clear, fluent, forceful, and articulate. Evoke imagery and speak with an upbeat tempo, but occasionally slow down for tension or emphasis.[8]

In contrast, Ronald Riggio took the second approach, and his research led him to recognize the significance of social skills. He identified six critical components of charisma:

- *Emotional expressivity*—the ability to express emotions

- *Emotional sensitivity*—the ability to feel the emotions of others

- *Emotional control*—the ability to control the outward display of inner emotions

- *Social expressivity*—the ability to express oneself

- *Social sensitivity*—understanding the social rules of
  the culture

- *Social control*—skill at role-playing

For each, he designed instruments to measure a leader's "charisma quotient," and then exercises the leader could practice to develop charisma and raise that quotient.[9]

Drucker took the third approach ("determine what charismatics do"), although he did not call it that. He noted that maximum effectiveness in dealing with others required definite attitudes and methods and cautioned that people were not simply machines to be managed without consideration of their human characteristics, motivations, and foibles.[10] He pointed out that this interaction was a two-way, not a one-way, relationship.[11]

Drucker showed that charisma is based on a leader's reaction to individuals and their reaction to the leader in applying certain social skills, in certain ways, in dealing with others, and he told leaders, in his own way, what to do to develop charisma.

Drucker's refined his ideas and recommendations. Different people have to be led differently.[12] Groups of people were each to be led differently.[13] Though this may appear obvious, it is not. Neither is it new, yet some leadership experts emphasize that individuals must be treated identically.

Captain Adolph von Schell served in combat throughout World War I in the Imperial German Army. In the early 1930s, his thesis, *Battle Leadership*, written while attending the Advanced Class of the U.S. Infantry School at Ft. Benning, Georgia, on leadership psychology, shows the importance of knowing and understanding your subordinates and, as Drucker said, treating them differently. Wrote von Schell, "We must know the probable reaction of the individual and the means by which we can influence this reaction."[14]

Drucker recommended that workers must be led differently at different times, again an important element of charisma.[15] Von Schell wrote the same thing in his book sixty years earlier:

"It is comparatively easy to make a correct estimate if one knows the man concerned; but even then it is often difficult, because the man doesn't always remain the same. He is no machine; he may react one way today, another way tomorrow. Soldiers can be brave one day and afraid the next. Soldiers are not machines but human beings who must be led in war. Each one of them reacts *differently* at *different* times, and must be handled *each time* according to his particular reaction. To sense this and to arrive at a correct psychological solution is part of the art of leadership."[16]

Drucker wrote emphatically that money alone does not motivate performance. Speaking of knowledge workers, he wrote, "They need, above all, challenge. They need to know the organization's mission and to believe in it."[17] In 1779 at the siege of Savannah during our Revolutionary War, Franco-American forces faced heavy English fire. Colonel Arthur Dillon offered his men of the LXXX Infanterie of the Franco-American force a hundred guineas to the first man to plant a flag in the British position. Not one man came forward. The colonel grew angry, and called his men cowards. Then one of his subordinates, a sergeant-major, couldn't contain himself. "If you hadn't offered money as an incentive, every man would have been willing to go," he shouted angrily at his superior officer. So saying, the sergeant-major got in front of the group and led it himself, and to a man the LXXX Infanterie followed and advanced against the English fire, achieving the desired result.[18]

Drucker on Charisma as a Motivator

Though he did not say how to apply these actions, Peter recommended that the leader motivate by several actions clearly characteristic of a charismatic leader:

- Lead, don't manage.

- Know who you are leading.

- Treat each individual differently depending on what motivates each.

- Treat groups differently depending on what motivates each.

- Lead individuals and groups differently, at different times, depending on the situation.

- Remember that those led need to know the organization's mission and to believe in it.

Leaders should heed Drucker's warning not to become misleaders, but charisma, whatever it is called, is useful as a component of Drucker's requirement to lead and motivate workers to peak performance.

CHAPTER 19

The Volunteer Paradigm

Drucker spent the last fifteen to twenty years of his life focused on nonprofit organizations, many of which had more volunteers than paid employees. From his experience with these organizations and their members, he formulated a concept that he articulated in *Management Challenges for the Twenty-First Century*, where he stated that full-time employees must be managed as if they were volunteers.

This may have been based on his observation of nonprofit organizations where paid workers and volunteers were treated identically. He reasoned that the workplace, even in non-volunteer-staffed corporations, had changed to such an extent that a complete makeover in how workers were treated and motivated was needed. He noted that pay was no longer the main motivator except under extreme economic circumstances. "We have known for fifty years that money alone does not motivate to perform," he wrote.

Change was necessary because, unlike their counterparts in the past, knowledge workers had mobility; they could leave one firm and go elsewhere with relative ease. Moreover, they had their own means of production, that is, their knowledge. From these facts, he concluded that what motivates unpaid volunteers should be used to motivate regular full-time employees.[1]

Drucker was correct about the power of how volunteers were treated to motivate. Again, he had tapped into something that was not necessarily new, but that had not yet been thought through. If anything, I think Drucker may have underestimated the power of volunteer treatment as a motivator. In a study of special military operations over the centuries, I found that while volunteer high-risk military organizations demanded much of their membership, they treated members differently—much better—than other military units, but not with high pay:

"The personnel in all commando units are especially selected and specially trained. The standards demanded of them are unbelievably high. The risks and hardships they face in their 'work' are supreme. The workload is probably more difficult and significantly greater than any other profession, military or otherwise. Yet, these special people volunteer, take immense risks and willingly do the impossible for pay and benefits that are almost trivial considering the effort required and the potential payoff."[2]

Drucker was on to something. However, while Drucker told us we should treat paid employees as if they were volunteers, he did not specify exactly how volunteers should be treated. For this, we must turn to research to explain what brings people to volunteer, and keep volunteering.

Why People Volunteer

To harness this powerful motivational force, it is important first to understand why men and women volunteer for work and then why they continue to do this work, be it dangerous, boring, difficult, or simply work that needs to be accomplished. One study at Michigan State University identified eight reasons why people volunteer:[3]

- To make a difference
- To use a talent or skill

- To gain professional experience or make contacts

- To express religious faith

- To meet people

- To achieve personal growth and enhanced self-esteem

- To seek a more balanced life

- To give something back

Another study linked beliefs with volunteer behavior. Six functions of behavior were identified:[4]

Values: To express humanitarian and pro-social values through action

Career: To explore career options and increase the likelihood that a particular career path can be pursued

Understanding: To gain greater understanding of the world, the diverse people in it, and ultimately, oneself

Enhancement: To boost self-esteem, to feel important and needed by others, and to form new friendships

Protective: To distract oneself from personal problems or to work through problems in the context of service

Social: To satisfy the expectations of friends and other close associates

While reasons for volunteering provide some insight for recruitment, if workers are to be treated as volunteers, it's necessary to know what causes volunteers to continue to volunteer after work has begun. One interesting study of volunteer workers identified a number of factors as important to retention in any volunteer job. The top ten were "helping others," "clearly defined responsibilities," "interesting work," "competence of supervisor," "supervisor guidance," "seeing results of my work," "working with a respected community organization," "reasonable work schedule," "doing the things I do best," and "suitable workload."[5] It doesn't take much imagination to see that these factors would motivate employees in the corporate world as well.

Social scientists have studied many corporations and industries to determine what factors employees consider most important in their jobs and therefore what motivates them to peak performance. Another important study was done by the Public Agenda Foundation and reported by John Naisbitt and Patricia Aburdene.[6] My wife, a clinical psychologist, says this basic research started more than fifty years ago and similar studies have been done with tens of thousands of workers in many industries, always with similar results. For almost twenty years, I have been using a form of this research to show that leaders and workers frequently have an entirely different perspective on the top motivational factors.

I ask my seminar attendees what they think the most important factors in motivating workers are—that is, what workers really want from their jobs. Then we compare their responses with the results received from workers over the years. Almost invariably, the results are not the same. Ranked by most important to least important, managers and supervisors have it almost backwards. The top ten results from workers (from the study mentioned earlier):

1. Work with people who treat me with respect

2. Interesting work

3. Recognition for good work

4. Chance to develop skills

5. Work for people who listen if you have ideas about how to do things better

6. Chance to think for myself rather than just carry out instructions

7. Seeing the end results of my work

8. Working for efficient managers

9. A job that is not too easy

10. Feeling well informed about what is going on

Many leaders and supervisors put job security, high pay, and good benefits at the top their lists. Notice that these three aren't even in the top ten of the study of what workers really want (though they are in the top fourteen). Other studies confirm these results.[7]

Drucker did not cite any of these studies, but he would have recognized that this was hardly breakthrough research. Abraham H. Maslow pointed out that as a lower need is satisfied it becomes less and less important, and the next need in the hierarchy becomes increasingly important. Maslow put economic want at the bottom or near bottom of his hierarchy and self-fulfillment at the top. Drucker was well acquainted with Maslow and cited his theories to make his point.[8]

Despite this, a typical response from my seminar attendees after seeing these results and having them explained is, "Not in my company!" I ask them to be open to the possibility that job security, high pay, and good benefits might not be as important in motivating their workers as they might have thought, since the top ten worker motivations cost a lot less and are usually much easier to provide.

It is interesting to compare the two studies of volunteer retention in non-paid positions with what full-time paid workers really want in their jobs. Interesting work is ranked high on both lists; number three on the volunteer list and number two on the paid worker list. In fact, eight out of ten items on the paid worker list are stated explicitly on the volunteer list. One could argue that the other two are implicit. Again, most of these cost very little.

The following sections take a look at each item to understand how it might be applied in the context of treating paid employees as if they were volunteer workers. Note how many of these are not only identical to research in volunteer motivation, but are consistent with Maslow's theories, which helps explain Drucker's concept: treat full-time paid employees as if they were volunteers.

1. Work with People Who Treat Me with Respect

Treating workers with respect has to do with their self-esteem. Failure to treat workers with respect lowers self-esteem and consequently depresses morale. This reduces the ability of the knowledge worker to achieve peak performance, and probably arouses bad feelings that at best contribute to a much lower performance level.

2. Interesting Work

It is truly amazing what people will do, at great cost and risk, if the work is truly interesting. The History Channel documented a recent explorer's search for Paititi, the lost Incan city of gold. The young explorer claimed that he searched primarily for fame and fortune, but the cost of the expedition in time, money, hardship, and risk of life hardly justified the tremendous expenditure of effort. The prize itself was uncertain, since, if found, it was sure to be claimed by one or more South American governments. Yet, he and several companions made not one but two expeditions, each lasting months in the rugged terrain of the mountainous Andes forests, fighting terrain, hostile natives, and disease. I have seen people in many industries work with little food or sleep to accomplish some goal that would have meant very little to very few because to them, their work regardless of situational variables was interesting.

3. Recognition for Good Work

Everyone wants recognition for work performed well. This does not mean undeserved recognition. Those led know the difference. Leaders who give compliments mistakenly believing that this act and false words will somehow motivate employees to high achievement are due for disappointment and worse. Workers know the difference. Not only will false praise engender lack of respect and trust in what a leader says, it will make it impossible for a leader to pay deserved compliments. A leader may encourage workers to do better, but needs to speak the truth.

This is somewhat different during the learning process, which I'll discuss in the context of the need for continuous training. One does not expect excellent performance from someone who is new to the job. With any human endeavor requiring any skill set, be it mental, physical, spiritual, or some mixture thereof, we start out with nothing. An infant doesn't begin two-legged mobility by running a marathon. Just standing is a chore and cause for celebration. Similarly with the first steps that are taken. Therefore, in the learning process and during training we are looking for effort and improvement rather than the peak performance eventually expected. By the same token, it is counterproductive to congratulate trained employees for a job not well done.

4. Chance to Develop Skills

Humans are proud of their development of skills, whatever they are. This is motivating. However, the leader should be closely involved with one important aspect. While skills can be developed by simply doing the task, people learn much faster by first being shown what to do and how to do it and then receiving help to correct errors and improve their skill. Continuous training is needed to provide a chance to develop skills and, for this reason, most major organizations rightly spend scarce resources on continuous training for their employees. If anything, this training and the opportunities to develop the skills of all should be increased.

5. Working for People Who Listen to Ideas for Improvement

Leading for peak performance is a two-way street. The leader has direct contact with the next highest level of management and is better able to see the operation overall and how employees are working together to accomplish the mission of the organization.

However, in every case the worker is on the firing line and knows more than the boss about what is going on at this level. Drucker believed in the critical importance of this symbiotic relationship.

Moreover, failing to listen is recognized by workers as a sign of either leader ignorance or disrespect of the employee's ideas. Everyone is deserving of respect and may have something to teach, even if not directly in line with their present work.

I recently learned of leadership lessons taught by a janitor who worked at the Air Force Academy in Colorado Springs. Bill Crawford was quiet, soft-spoken, and ignored by all. The cadets thought, "Bill is an old man working in a young person's world. What does he have to offer us on a personal level?"

One day a cadet read in a military history book that Crawford had won the Congressional Medal of Honor, the nation's highest award for bravery, during World War II. Crawford, an infantry private fighting in Italy under intense enemy fire and on his own initiative, had single-handedly attacked a well-fortified enemy position. Only then did the cadets begin to listen to what Crawford said. What they learned was so valuable that a former cadet, now a full colonel and senior commander, wrote an article about the leadership lessons learned from this janitor and former Army private. Colonel Moschgat wrote: "I spent four years at the Air Force Academy, took dozens of classes, read hundreds of books, and met thousands of great people. I gleaned leadership skills from all of them, but one of the people I remember most is Mr. Bill Crawford and the lessons he unknowingly taught. Don't miss your opportunity to learn."[9]

6. A Chance to Think for Myself

Workers want to be involved in decision making. Drucker cautioned that this was necessary for knowledge workers or they could not do their best. Research has certainly confirmed this. At Strathclyde University in Glasgow, researchers looked at sixty-three organizations that had implemented a new performance-related payment system. The study took three years, and the results showed that organizations could succeed or fail using exactly the same system and methods of implementation. In fact, two-thirds of the organizations studied failed with the new system and only a third succeeded. The only factor that correlated well with these results was something called "involvement/consultation," which was defined as the amount of time and effort that leaders spent discussing the proposed new system with their employees and with other subordinate managers before the system's introduction. In this way, those who implemented the system had a chance to work out the problems by thinking for themselves. Drucker said workers need to have some control and freedom in their work situation.[10] As Peter pointed out, people are not passive receivers of motivational stimuli, even if the goals of the top leader are worthy and the systems to be implemented well-thought-through and flawless.

7. Seeing the End Results of My Work

Many of these motivational factors fit together. Workers want to know what will be done with their work and how it fits into the overall mission. Drucker wrote of the importance of a mission that all members of an organization could believe in. I would add that it must be communicated succinctly and understandably. I liked the way that John F. Kennedy said, "We choose to go to the moon!"

Churchill's famous "blood, toil, tears, and sweat" is in the same category. This was Churchill's first speech as prime minister and was delivered on May 13, 1940, when Hitler had invaded France and was in the process of defeating the combined British Expeditionary Force and French armies, which he did a month later. Churchill said:

> I would say to the House, as I said to those who have joined this Government, I have nothing to offer but blood, toil, tears and sweat. We have before us an ordeal of the most grievous kind. We have before us many long months of toil and struggle.

You ask what is our policy. I will say, it is to wage war with all our might, with all the strength that God can give us, to wage war against a monstrous tyranny never surpassed in the dark, lamentable catalogue of human crime.

You ask what is our aim? I can answer in one word: Victory. Victory at all costs. Victory in spite of all terror. Victory however long and hard the road may be. For without victory there is no survival.

Both speeches were very effective. The United States reached the moon within a decade, although at the time of Kennedy's speech, its space program lagged behind that of the Soviet Union, and, of course, Britain did prevail over Germany after many defeats and setbacks. It is also worth pointing out that in both speeches the results desired were very clear.

How the mission will be accomplished is usually replete with challenges and reaching the intended goal is frequently far from easy. However, none of the people charged with completing the mission, whether as part of a nation or as part of another organization, want intermediate results sugarcoated. They want to know what's going on and how they are doing. Of course, if all the news is bad, without any indication of success, you will have problems. Volunteers and paid employees need to see results, by which Drucker meant positive results, for their effort.[11]

8. Working for Efficient Managers

A friend of my wife's was a practicing clinical psychologist with more than twenty years' experience. Between her income and her husband's, finances were no longer a factor. Earlier in her career, she had wanted to work for a nonprofit institution, but the pay was low, and, because her husband was just getting started, she could not afford to do this. Since this was no longer the situation, she gave up her practice and went to work for a nationally recognized nonprofit at something like 25 percent of her former earnings. She looked forward to contributing to those who would not normally be able to afford her services. Her enthusiasm soon vanished as she saw an inefficient boss waste human resources, herself and others. Within six months, she resigned and found another organization in which to contribute.

9. A Job That Is Not Too Easy

It is a fact that workers don't want tasks that are so easy that anyone can accomplish them. They need a challenge. That doesn't mean every task must be nearly impossible. A series of failures, despite good efforts, is not motivating. However, an occasional joust against "impossible" odds is worthwhile, and victory is a tremendous motivational boost. I once saw a young chief engineer assume the task of winning a major contract against a much stronger, established competitor in a field that his organization had not yet entered. It wasn't easy, and it took two years, but when winning it propelled his organization to a long string of victories.

Upon reading about this successful struggle, Hilary Powers, one of my editors, told me about an example she experienced on the other end of the scale. She once worked for an organization that had had endless trouble with its ammonia-based Ozalid copying equipment. None of the operators hired to run this equipment seemed to care much about the job or anything else. Malfunctions were constant, and in her words, when they did manage to produce copies, they provided "service with a snarl." Then a personnel manager got the brilliant idea of hiring a couple of people with below normal IQs. They were immediately interested in the job, and it showed. Not only did the problems stop and service improve, but according to Hilary, these were the happiest and most gracious people in the building—a bonus that further improved everyone's productivity.

10. Feeling Well Informed About What Is Going On

Without full information, a worker cannot accept responsibility for peak performance or for making rapid changes unsupervised when required and a leader cannot lead effectively. While I phrase this as *"feeling* well informed," workers and subordinate leaders must *be* well informed or they cannot reach peak performance.

Drucker on Treating Employees as Volunteers

Drucker believed that the productivity of the knowledge worker was likely to become central to the management of people, just as productivity of the manual worker was central to managing people a hundred years ago. He knew this would require very different assumptions about what motivates people in their organizations and necessitate that we treat regular workers as if they were volunteers.[12] This chapter identifies a number of reasons why people volunteer, as well as important factors that people want from their paid jobs. It is striking to see the similarity between the two lists, and how this similarity supports Drucker's recommendations on this aspect of motivation.

PART FIVE

The Marketing Model of Leadership

Thus far, I have concentrated on "Drucker on Leadership," that is, Drucker's own ideas, concepts, and principles. I have documented his thoughts, and noted if and how these changed, as well as where I filled in the blanks.

This section is different. Drucker stated unequivocally that leadership was "a marketing job"; however, he did little to develop this concept. He did not define a marketing job or explain how to apply marketing thought to leadership. This section begins with Drucker's views and continues with my interpretation of where his concepts lead.

Marketing as a leadership concept probably is Drucker's most audacious idea in the field. By this, he did not mean that leadership should be manipulative, a belief I'm afraid many executives hold even without the marketing model, much to the detriment of themselves, their organizations, and those they lead. It is worth recalling that Drucker defined leadership in these terms:

"Leadership is the lifting of a man's vision to higher sights, the raising of a man's performance to a higher standard, the building of a man's personality beyond its normal limitations."[1]

Some who do not deal in marketing directly hold on to another very old but incorrect notion: that marketing is just a fancy word for selling and that the two are identical. In Drucker-like fashion, Peter explained the difference in a statement that, while true, was designed to provoke both thought and controversy. "The objective of marketing," he said, "is to make selling superfluous."[2] (More about this in Chapter Twenty.)

In the late 1980s, I concluded that leadership and salesmanship shared a common and important element—persuasion. I examined literature in both disciplines and was amazed at the similarities in goals and the techniques used to persuade, and concluded that good salespeople were also leaders, and good leaders frequently employed techniques used by good and ethical salespeople.

Then Peter published *Management Challenges for the Twenty-First Century*. In a chapter titled "Management's New Paradigms," he restated many of the ideas he spoke of years earlier, including the idea of treating all workers as if they were volunteers (see Chapter Nineteen). He went even further and called workers "partners," and wrote that partners couldn't simply be ordered around—they had to be persuaded. My first thought was, "Did I actually anticipate Drucker in this insight?" Maybe. However, Peter went further and left me in the dust. Since "partners" had to be persuaded, leadership was "a marketing job."[3] This got me thinking. I knew he didn't mean any kind of manipulation, which would have gone against all of his beliefs. What then did Drucker mean by "a marketing job"?

Modern marketing rests on something called the "marketing concept." The basis of the marketing concept is that firms should seek to discover and then satisfy the needs of their customers rather than persuade customers to purchase existing products or services in which they might not be interested. Since Drucker taught that if marketing were done perfectly, selling would be unnecessary, to practice marketing correctly, it would be necessary to understand the needs of each group or customer segment, including their values and behaviors, so as to approach them in their preferred manner and allow them to relate to the product or service without interference. In Drucker's terms, if the marketing aspect of leadership were done perfectly, the persuasion element would be unnecessary. I recalled Xenophon's description of Cyrus the Great's leadership, which was so powerful that one king defeated by him, on his own initiative, paid twice the tribute Cyrus asked. Drucker was on to something. In this final section, I present my adaptation of Drucker's revolutionary and bold concept.

CHAPTER 20

Applying Marketing to Leadership

Perhaps Drucker's greatest leadership gift is one of his least known but also one of his most far-reaching and integrative ideas: good leadership is essentially marketing. This concept is based on Peter's view that all knowledge workers are partners in an organization, and therefore cannot simply be ordered around. They must be led, and leadership, Drucker concluded, was a marketing job.[1]

I had previously looked at the necessity for persuasion in both salesmanship and leadership. However, Drucker did not say "salesmanship"; he said "marketing." I immediately understood exactly what he meant, and was awed by his genius and his ability to integrate facts and theories from different disciplines to arrive at conclusions that seem obvious. Of course, they only seem obvious after Drucker states them.

Note again, that Drucker did not say that leadership was "a selling job." He said "a marketing job." This is an important difference.

After eleven years of Air Force service, I resigned my regular Air Force commission and lived abroad for three years. On my return I sought a job in research and development. However, one CEO who interviewed me for the second time asked if I would be interested in a position in marketing. I declined, saying that I knew little about selling. He immediately explained that he did not want me for a position having to do with selling, but for marketing—which was entirely different. He wanted me to look at who his buyers were. He wanted to know how they thought and how best to reach them with the company's offerings. He further wanted to know what these potential buyers valued and wanted. He wanted me to look at what products the company produced or could produce would be most desired by these potential buyers and how best to get these products to them. He wanted to know all this and a lot more.

The closest this came to selling was that he wanted to know what kind of sales force might be needed or whether engineers should do the selling themselves, since this was a high-tech product bought by large organizations. In the end I didn't take the job, and was offered a job as director of research and development, my original goal, at another company. However, I did learn from this incident that marketing and selling were not the same.

The Difference Between Marketing and Selling

Drucker wrote that not only is marketing not selling, the two are not even complementary. Many marketing experts might disagree with this; but, before I examine this claim, let's look first at marketing. Famed marketing professor Philip Kotler has said that if he can be called "the father of marketing," then Peter Drucker is "the grandfather of marketing."[2] Indeed, Drucker had a long history of exploring the mysteries of marketing. In his first book devoted to management, Drucker wrote that there are only two basic functions of business: marketing and innovation, and that any organization in which marketing is either absent or incidental is not a business.[3]

Thirty-six years later, in a detailed interview with Kotler included in Managing the Nonprofit Organization, he made clear that marketing was not just a concept for business but for other organizations as well.[4] Drucker wrote that marketing "is the whole business seen from the point of view of the final result, that is, from the customer's point of view. Concern and responsibility for marketing must therefore permeate all areas of the enterprise."[5]

Not only did Drucker say that marketing was far broader than selling, he also maintained that "selling and marketing were antithetical rather than synonymous or complementary."[6] Even today, most textbooks describe selling as a subset of marketing. How then could it be antithetical to marketing?

To Drucker, marketing was concerned with top-level thinking, decision making, and strategies. There were various means of carrying out these strategies: advertising, selling, pricing, and distribution, among others. We refer to techniques used to implement strategies as *tactics*. Tactics and strategies are not the same, as discussed in Chapter Fifteen. Strategy is far more important; in fact, your tactics may be less than perfect, but if your strategy is correct, you can still be successful. General Robert E. Wood, CEO of Sears Roebuck during its period of greatest growth, said, "Business is like war in one respect—if its grand strategy is correct, any number of tactical errors can be made, and yet the enterprise proves successful."[7] Let's see why this is so.

You may remember the XFL, a football league that lasted only one season back in 2001. The XFL itself was the brainchild of Vince McMahon, World Wrestling Federation chairman. The idea was to combine the sport of football with pure spectacle as had been done with wrestling. McMahon thought that he could duplicate the success that professional wrestling had enjoyed over the years. His basic strategy was to offer this new spectacle as "off-season football," an additional advantage being that it would not compete with games conducted during the regular season. In fact, according to McMahon it would attract football fans hungry for football after the regular season was over. The problem was that the strategy was wrong and McMahon didn't understand that the market segment he wanted to appeal to was entirely different from the one with which he was familiar. McMahon was ridiculed by mainstream sports journalists due to the stigma attached to professional wrestling's image as being "fake." Some sports journalists speculated, only half-jokingly, whether any of the league's games were rigged for one side or the other. For the same reason, regular football fans were unconvinced from the start.

So much for the strategy; that is, so much for marketing. The tactics were pretty good. Good TV coverage, including NBC, who was a partner, no penalties for roughness, and fewer rules in general. This was intended to liven things up and contribute to the spectacle, almost like Roman gladiators reborn. The teams played their hearts out, and many of the players went on (or back) to the NFL once the league broke up. And presumably those on the sales end sold their hearts out. But that's all tactics. Great tactics were well executed, but the strategy was in error.

Specifically relating this to selling versus marketing, marketing is strategic, selling is tactical. The greatest salesperson in the world may do a fantastic job in selling the wrong product or service to the wrong buyer. If successful, the sales enable management to continue with the wrong strategy, whereas if the effort failed outright, management might be forced to develop a winning strategy and a lot more product might be sold with less effort. In this way, selling and marketing can be antithetical. This is important for leadership. Get the strategy (that is, the marketing) right, and you may succeed even with tactical errors.

During World War II, a major leadership study of more than a million soldiers showed that the number one trait they wanted to see in their leaders was competence, above all else.[8] Competence can be viewed as a major leadership strategy. Get that right, and you can do a lot of other things wrong. Not that you should, but you can. And that wasn't just true in our army during World War II, either. Also during World War II, an experienced German military leader said the same thing.

Captain Wolfgang Luth of the German Navy spoke to a graduating class of naval cadets. Captain Luth was one of the most successful submarine commanders in the German submarine force. During World War II, thirty-nine thousand officers and men served in Germany's U-boats. Only about seven thousand survived. If you saw the award-winning movie *Das Boot*, you know under what difficult conditions these men, and those of our own submarine force, served and fought. Just surviving a U-boat patrol was a severe challenge for any leader. Yet, beyond mere survival, during three years of war, Luth led twelve patrols and sank close to 250,000 gross tons of shipping. He was 600 days at sea in his submarine during this period, spending a record-setting 203 days at sea on just one patrol. Not surprisingly, this amazing submarine captain held Germany's highest decorations for valor. Luth's topic for these future naval officers was leadership on a U-boat. Captain Luth covered many areas in his lecture: the dos and don'ts, the life of the submariner, discipline. At times he indicated that the captain's actions were matters of judgment—that a different commander might have acted differently and still been successful. On one aspect of leadership, however, he said there was only one right answer. "Crews will always prefer the successful commander, even though he may be a fathead, to the one who is consideration itself, but sinks no ships," he stated.[9] Like the U.S. Army study demonstrated, Captain Luth found that, above all, a leader had to be competent.

This is what I called "knowing your stuff" in the study that I did, described in Chapter Fourteen. "Knowing your stuff" or competence was an overall, encompassing strategy that might be supported by a tactic we could term "consideration." Both the strategy of competence and the tactics of consideration are part of marketing.

The Rise of Marketing

Marketing and leadership seem to have little in common. Even their basic development differed greatly. To Drucker, leadership's basic principles were thought through, tried, optimized, well established (known by the ancients millennia ago), and documented in books. He saw marketing as a relatively recent development. He agreed with the orthodox accounts of the development of marketing as production evolved from handcraft to manufacturing. Take books, for example, prepared laboriously by skilled scribes, who frequently spent more time transcribing the work than the author did writing it. One error could destroy many weeks of work since an entire page would need to be redone. A single book might take a year or more of labor by these trained specialists. There was no need for marketing. Bookselling was an engineering and production issue.

These ancient processes were revolutionized by technology and the Industrial Revolution, which made books available to almost everyone at relatively low cost. As competition entered the marketplace and overproduction created the need to get rid of inventory, being able to sell the product produced became an issue.

Drucker claimed that the Japanese developed marketing in the seventeenth century. A merchant came to Tokyo with a revolutionary concept of selling. Previously, all selling was done by the manufacturers themselves, who made or grew what they sold. This merchant didn't sell a single class of goods. He sold all kinds of goods, mostly made by others. He was essentially a buying agent, who saw his task not as persuading others to purchase a product he had on hand and had to sell, but rather to discover first what his customers wanted and then get these desired products from others.

To be successful, this retailer had to research the market and have products that the consumer wanted first, or he would soon have gone out of business. Other aspects of marketing have grown up since, but the basic idea of having what the customer wants rather than selling what you had to an unsuspecting customer was firmly established.[10] In a news interview with one of the judges on *American Idol*, the judge was asked to comment on the decline in sales in the recording industry at the same time as *American Idol* and its alumni had achieved great success. "That's easy," he said.

"The recording studios have been trying to give the public what they think the public wants. We let the public decide, and we then we give it to them." That is pure marketing!

The Value of Marketing as a Leadership Model

The American Marketing Association's definition of marketing is probably as good as any, or at least it has the general blessing of its membership, about forty thousand as of this writing, making it the largest marketing association in North America. According to the AMA, "Marketing is the activity, set of institutions, and processes for creating, communicating, delivering, and exchanging offerings that have value for customers, clients, partners, and society at large."[11]

This definition, approved in October 2007, is significant for leadership. Note especially the words "exchanging offerings that have value for customers. . . ." A political candidate in a democracy offers promises in exchange for a vote. In his successful bid for the presidency, Barack Obama offered "change" in exchange for a vote. This is a good example of both marketing and leadership.

An organizational leader also offers something to followers in exchange for followership. This may include organizational success, mission accomplishment, personal achievement, and so on. In Part Four, I discuss the many things that motivate the knowledge worker besides money. These can all be viewed as things offered in exchange for followership.

The marketing concept states that organizations must analyze the needs of their customers and then make better decisions than their competitors' to satisfy those needs. How this is done again relates back to what is offered in exchange for money, a vote, or, if leadership is "a marketing job" as Drucker indicated, in exchange for followership.

Certain elements are required, including focusing on the buyers and satisfying their individual wants and needs, viewing the entire organization as part of marketing, supporting the marketing effort, having what the buyers want, and attending to the welfare of both the buyers and society. This is the ideal. When organizations fall short, marketing is deemed less than optimal, and, in the case of lapses in considering buyer or societal welfare, even unethical or illegal. One can easily say the same about leadership.

How to Adopt Marketing as a Leadership Concept

As discussed in Part One, Peter Drucker believed, before all else, that the leader's primary responsibility is for the organization's future. Therefore, leaders must begin with a mission they believe in, one that is believable by those they lead. Making this mission believable, communicating and promoting it, is a continual process. At the same time, leaders must proceed to developing the strategies to reach the goals and objectives required to achieve, communicate, and promote that believable mission.

Various marketing concepts should be used to communicate, promote, and implement these strategies for creating the organization's future. One marketing concept, segmentation, is noteworthy here. Segmentation refers to categorizing a market using common characteristics that define the prospects' wants and needs or other qualities. This enables concentration on these markets and aspects of these markets to avoid spreading limited resources too thin in an attempt to sell to everyone, even though specialization might mean the loss of some marginal sales.

Positioning is similar to differentiation, that is, how your organization differs from others, but it is far more powerful. It has to do with communicating your unique position to a sometimes jaded following. Marketing experts Al Ries and Jack Trout wrote a best seller, *Positioning: The Battle for Your Mind*, which created, or at least popularized, the concept—and revolutionized marketing.[12] Positioning, along with segmentation, is a powerful strategy. In the following chapters, I discuss these and other marketing concepts and their application to leadership.

CHAPTER 21

Applying Segmentation to Leadership

Segmentation is a strategic concept in marketing. What does it do for a leader? You might think that the best strategy for any type of communication as a marketer (or a leader) is to appeal to everyone at once, which implies an identical message presented identically at the same time. That is, not to segment at all. The biggest advantage of mass marketing is the economies of scale that come from communicating with a potentially huge market in this way. If everyone in the United States is considered a candidate for a product, it's a market of several hundred million. Go worldwide, and you're talking several billion. Unfortunately, mass marketing is not actually a good idea in all situations, whether within marketing or leadership.

Disadvantages of Mass Marketing

A mass-marketing strategy begins with the assumption that all individuals in this market think and act alike, and are identical in other ways as well. While this assumption is usually incorrect, there may be such a thing as a "mass mind," but that is unusual (see Chapter Twenty-Three). As Xenophon, Drucker, and Captain von Schell have made plain, for the most part those we lead are not at all alike.

For mass marketing to be effective, the product or service and environment would have to be such that the desire or need is the same and that it is perceived identically by all ages, incomes, geographic locations, and cultures. Certain basic commodities— electricity, gas, or water, for example—may have these attributes. However, even with such commodities, issues of belief, religion, culture, or national honor may mean that communications about these products cannot be identical. Approaches you might think of as no-brainers may provide unpleasant surprises if you try them with some groups.

The members of a tribe living in the jungles of South America have very short life spans due to a disease that is common and unique to them. Government scientists investigated and found that the disease and early deaths were due to a microscopic worm that lived in the particular wood from which these people build their huts. Simple solutions to the problem: don't build homes using this type of wood, or move to another location, or both. This was explained to the tribe. Problem solved, right? Wrong. The location and the wood are integral to custom, culture, and religion. The people understood the issue perfectly, but preferred doing what they'd always done and staying in the same place. The scientists had to find another solution. Clearly all people are not the same and must be led differently.

The Solution for Marketers and Leaders: Segmentation

Segmentation refers to categorizing a market by common features, which define wants, needs, and any other critical characteristics. This is a very important concept that researchers discovered on the firing line over the years. You can't be everything to everybody.

Different markets and people have different wants, needs, values, and interests. Recently my wife and I were at an upscale department store in an expensive part of town looking for a particular china pattern. We found one that was close, but decided that it wasn't quite what we wanted. We decided to look elsewhere.

On the way home, we stopped to buy kitchen cleanser at an entirely different type of retail outlet located in a shopping center. It was a national brand store, known primarily for value, not upscale merchandise. We certainly weren't looking for china. To our surprise, we noticed that the store sold china. Even more surprising, we saw the exact brand of imported china that we had deemed "close" at about 50 percent of the upscale store's price.

Why the price difference? Those who shop at the upscale store do so because of its image for high-quality and frequently exclusive merchandise. This china appeared to be of high quality. The wholesale cost to both stores was probably identical, or nearly so. However, for the upscale department store a low price would seem incongruous with high quality and exclusivity unless it was a special sale. At a low price, they might not have sold much (or much more), and in any case it would have hurt the store's exclusive image to present such an offering. In any case, the upscale department store felt that the china fit with its other product lines, so long as it charged a comparably high price. We thought it worth the money when we saw it there, and we seriously considered buying the set.

The other store sold value merchandise, be it kitchen cleanser or china. As long as it was perceived as good value and sold at a relatively low price, the product would sell. The wholesale price paid allowed the retailer to charge a price that fit its general "good value for the money" image.

Here we have an identical product selling at two entirely different retail outlets at considerably different prices. The demographics and the expectations of the customers at both stores are different. Had the two stores chosen an identical selling price, one that was simultaneously perceptibly higher than the standard fare of the value store and lower than that of the upscale department store, probably neither would have sold the product successfully.

Segmentation has other advantages for a marketer. By concentrating efforts on one or more selected parts of the market, a marketer can concentrate on the things that are most important to the individuals in these market sections. This is a fundamental principle of all strategy, not just marketing strategy. In this way, a marketer avoids spreading resources, which are always limited, over all markets. It means being strong in a limited number of segments as opposed to being weak everywhere.

What Segmentation Means for the Leader

Segmentation coincides with Drucker's belief that human beings are different and must be treated differently. The 2008 presidential election provides a useful example of how different groups of people are approached differently.

The United States is made up of a host of different cultures, geographic areas, religions, occupations, and other divisions. Even though there are certain common interests, these different segments must be approached differently. Both candidates tried to do this.

The concept of appealing to different groups in their preferred way and in accordance with their interests is correct. However, the leader must be careful to maintain a consistent story, even if the story is presented with a different emphasis to different groups. Barack Obama, for example, told a group of American Jews that Jerusalem should remain the undivided capital of Israel and intimated that he intended to move the American Embassy in Israel from Tel Aviv to Jerusalem. Speaking on CNN the next day, he "clarified" and modified his stance significantly. Even after winning the election, he is still facing criticism for his apparent flip-flopping.[1]

What the leader or marketer says or promises can't change with different groups or the leader loses credibility. This is easier with smaller groups, more difficult with larger groups located around the country or around the world.

The Basics of One-on-One Segmentation

In 1987, three of my students won an award sponsored by the Philip Morris Corporation for a marketing plan they developed. They and I were invited to New York City to receive the award. Among five other groups of students similarly honored was one led by a young communications professor, Martha Rogers. Little did I know that six years later Martha would catapult to the top of the best-seller list with her partner, Don Peppers, with a book called *The One to One Future*.[2] Like most revolutionary concepts, the basic idea is simple. It is to concentrate on providing services or products to one customer at a time by identifying and then meeting their individual needs. It then aims to repeat this many times with each customer, thereby forging powerful lifelong relationships. This is one-on-one segmentation and it is a near-perfect example of segmentation and the marketing approach to leadership.

The more you know about those you lead, the better, and only with full knowledge can you can lead them well. The bare basics are each person's name, family, and facts about their life and interests. Drucker followed his own advice in this. I was surprised at how much Drucker knew about each of his students. My wife, Nurit, met Peter at the first party at the beginning of my first year. I'm sure he met many people that evening. He spoke with her a few minutes and then went on. The following year, we again attended the annual party. At one point, Nurit saw Peter and went to greet him, saying only, "You probably won't remember me, but—" Before she could finish, he replied, "Of course I do. You're Nurit Cohen, Bill Cohen's wife."

One head of a senior government school memorized the names of all of his new officer-students, members of their families, and their general interests from a book with photographs and names that had been mailed out to incoming students. At their first social gathering, he greeted more than three hundred attendees—every officer and family member—by name and was able to say a few words about something of interest to each although he had met few of them.

To say this impressed these senior officers is an understatement. The following day he told his assembled students that in addition to wanting to meet their spouses, he had done this with instructional intent. First, he wanted to emphasize that all leaders must know everything they can about their subordinates. In addition, he wanted to prove that it could be done by any leader who was committed to do it, and without any special memory devices.

Maybe you don't need to go as far as this leader did to learn about the people you work and interact with or to prove a point. However, knowing and understanding people underlies Drucker's marketing approach to successful leadership.

Interacting with Staff in the Workplace

If Peter had interacted with his students only in the classroom, I doubt that he would have known them as well or had the same impact on them. Drucker never passed up the opportunity to interact with his students outside the classroom. He not only attended such university events as the beginning of school year party, he attended almost every school event to which he was invited—and he was invited to many. I have seen professors of far less stature than Peter who declined invitations from their own universities to participate in school activities, apparently because they considered themselves too important or too busy. Peter, a documented workaholic, was never too busy. Consequently his students interacted with him frequently, and he with them, even when not taking courses from him. This continued after graduation. In this way, Peter was able to stay abreast of his students' activities throughout their professional lives. It seems to me that, after I had graduated, every time we talked the first thing he wanted to know was what I was doing. Remember the one-to-one marketing concept as conceived by Peppers and Rogers. My relationship with Peter was a lifetime relationship because of his efforts as much as my own.

Drucker practiced what he preached. He knew that meeting people face-to-face and talking with them was essential to good leadership. Some years ago, Tom Peters and Robert Waterman popularized the technique they called MBWA ("management by wandering around").[3] This is not a new technique. Julius Caesar didn't call it that, but that's what he did. In politics and on the battlefield, he wandered around seeing for himself what was going on and learning the name of even the most junior subordinate. In modern times, successful senior executives have followed this model. Robert W. Galvin, CEO and later chairman of the board of Motorola, knew the value of getting to know his people. He told his managers, "I believe we in top management must circulate."[4] Under his leadership, Motorola's sales grew from $216.6 million to $6.7 billion. Douglas D. Danforth, then chairman of the board at Westinghouse, echoed his sentiment: "The better the CEO knows his key people personally, the better he will be able to correctly estimate their strengths."[5]

However, while wandering around, you need to be careful that you don't take authority away from the middle management leaders between you and the people you meet. Still, by seeing and being seen, you greatly increase the effectiveness of communications up and down the line. You learn what's right and what's wrong, which allows you to correct problems right away. You can dramatize your ideas and what your goals to your workers. That way the word gets around—fast.

Perhaps even more important, you learn more about who your people really are. A human being isn't only the owner of certain skills, possessor of a certain reputation that may or may not be deserved, recipient of a certain amount of money, and holder of a certain position in your organization. Any subordinate is much more: a man or woman of flesh and blood, someone's spouse, boyfriend or girlfriend, child, parent. Each has hopes, dreams, problems, victories, defeats, and opportunities. Each has unique qualities, abilities, capabilities, and limitations. Faced with a certain situation, each will usually react characteristically. Each has the potential to contribute much to your organization, or to commit errors that can drag your organization down and even cause it to fail.

Of course, you can't lead only by wandering around and talking with people. Simply walking around, as good a technique as it is, isn't the only way of interacting with those you lead at work. There are many job-related activities that cut across organizational lines and for which you do not need a permanent organization, including committees and teams created to solve specific problems, do planning, bid contracts, or handle any of a number of other activities. Many companies take on tasks that are primarily for the benefit of organizations outside the company. Some take place on the company's premises and on company time. Community fund drives and savings bonds drives are a couple of examples. It really doesn't matter where these activities are conducted. Many companies simply assign these tasks to an assistant or to the most junior member of the organization. To me that is a waste of an excellent opportunity to get to know, and give leadership experience, to some of your younger managers. It is also another opportunity to interact with and get to know those you lead.

Interacting with Staff Outside the Workplace

There are more ways to get to know your people, and many of these are activities you can initiate yourself or can assign others, depending on your position. These include social activities, professional activities, or some that are a combination of both. All of them help you observe and get to know your people in a wide variety of situations and allow an opportunity for one-on-one segmentation.

Many require a number of management and leadership roles, and that's good, too, because it gives you an opportunity to observe your people in action and see how they perform as leaders in different roles. I once worked for an executive who used such opportunities to test the leadership potential of the managers reporting to him.

Parties, such as those Drucker attended, are examples on internal social activities. However, they are but one example. There are also company picnics, sporting events, management clubs, retirement and award ceremonies, and more. All of these activities require someone to organize and run them. If your subordinates know that you use these activities to help you decide about future promotions, you'll probably have many who will volunteer for the jobs.

These activities provide powerful opportunities for you to learn more about those you lead, but you must be careful not to let them take your focus away from the organization's main mission. Done correctly, they can support the mission because by knowing and understanding your people well, you will be able to develop and make the best use of their talents.

Off-Duty and Unofficial Meetings

Sometimes they get it right on TV, sometimes not. If you watch TV even occasionally, you are familiar with the many dramas or sitcoms that center around lawyers, law enforcement, newsrooms, or other types of businesses or professions. Many of the scenes occur after work and socially in bars. What the television people get right is the amount of work done in these unofficial settings. Such meetings really do take place, and in these relaxed atmospheres, leaders get to know those who work for and with them.

Herb Kelleher was one of the most dynamic and charismatic CEOs of modern times. *Fortune* even suggested that perhaps he was the best CEO in America.[6] Kelleher probably came to know his people better than any other company leader at Southwest Airlines through his frequent after-work meetings with his employees at the bar. However, he never overlooked an opportunity, no matter what the setting.

At his retirement, the pilots' union took a full-page advertisement in *USA Today* thanking him for his job as CEO. Kelleher knew many of his thousands of employees and called them by their first names. Said one, "He's just the most fantastic and incredible leader. . . . He knows everyone." Kelleher actually hired one pilot, "Joe," at a 7–11.[7]

The Function of Segmentation in Leadership

Segmentation is as important in leadership as it is in marketing. It means knowing that every one of your followers is different, and you must know and understand these differences to lead them effectively. For communication purposes, segmentation of your employees is essential, especially in a large company. However, the objective is one-on-one segmentation and a lifetime relationship. This is what Drucker practiced, and this is in part what he meant by leadership being a marketing job.

CHAPTER 22

Applying Positioning to the Organization and the Leader

ositioning is a powerful concept originated by two advertising executives, Al Ries and Jack Trout. Jack Trout first published an article on positioning in 1969.[1] Three years later Ries and Trout together published a series of articles in *Advertising Age* called "The Positioning Era." The concept caught on almost immediately, and advertising and marketing executives began to develop positions and positioning slogans for their clients. *Positioning* has become part of the lexicon of marketing.

The Role of Positioning in Communication

Positioning has to do with the communication process and how to use that process effectively to persuade a target audience. For this reason, the two authors recognized that the concept was applicable not only to advertising and marketing but to any human activity requiring communication—that is, almost everything. Their book contains examples of positioning a company, a product, a service, a Long Island bank, a career, and even the Catholic Church and a country (Belgium in their example).

It is impossible to imagine leadership without communication, and the importance of communication in leadership is self-evident. Since leaders have been communicating with followers for thousands of years, however, what does the positioning concept add? Ries and Trout developed this concept in an attempt to answer the question, How does an advertiser (the sender) break through the hundreds of messages to get the consumer to believe its message and purchase a product?

They started with a well-established fact: the vast majority of advertising is wasted and ineffective. Exploring various psychological concepts, they realized that the important part of presenting an advertising message, any message, was not getting through to the prospect's mind. Rather, much depended on what was already in the mind of the prospect and the prospect's reaction to a new message. In the recent presidential election, Barack Obama introduced the message of "change" before his competitors in his campaign. It was an extremely powerful message used first in the campaign to win the nomination and then in the actual campaign for the presidency. Although Hillary Clinton had been the leading Democratic candidate and was expected to get the nomination of her party, she could not overcome a combination of Obama's charisma and his positioning. McCain, respected and trusted as he was, could not overcome Obama's positioning either, even when he attempted to challenge this position with a message of "real change" or "change you can trust."

In 1981, Ries and Trout authored a best-selling book, now a marketing classic: *Positioning: The Battle for Your Mind*. In it they wrote, "Positioning starts with a product. A piece of merchandise, a service, a company, an institution, or even a person. . . . But positioning is not what you do to a product. Positioning is what you do in the mind of the prospect. That is, you position the product in the mind of the prospect."[2]

The insight these two advertising mavens came up with was a blockbuster confirmed by psychological research, and it changed marketing, advertising, and persuasive communication forever. Now it is understood that the challenge in getting a message to an intended receptor in any communication is the predisposition to react to the message depending on filters and preloading constructed over a lifetime of experiences and values as well as recent occurrences in the person's environment.

Case Study: How to Apply Positioning to Leadership

Bob Cleeter was assigned to lead a prototype organization when the previous manufacturing manager, George Smith, was relieved of his duties. This prototype unit had been set up to confirm the integration of new machinery with high technology to result in high-speed production at very low cost under operational conditions. The high-tech machinery was extremely expensive and a good deal of money had been invested in assembling and testing the concept. It had already been proven in the lab and as a system, but had not been run by ordinary workers and managers in the operational environment. Once the system was confirmed, more units would be brought on line and it would then have the potential to pay back the company's investment many times over.

George Smith was highly competent and had done well in leading other company manufacturing organizations. In fact, he had been especially selected for this position. He was patient, unexcitable, and highly popular with those he led. He was well qualified technically. The entire manufacturing team had been given training deemed adequate and appropriate by the company that developed the equipment and designed the new manufacturing system.

Despite testing prior to establishing the experimental manufacturing organization, after several months trying to produce the company's standard products under operational conditions and Smith's leadership, it had failed miserably.

Each time, Smith analyzed what went wrong. It always seemed to be something different. Sometimes individual machines didn't perform as they should and it appeared to be a maintenance or reliability problem. At other times, human error fouled up procedures. It was always something. The system should work. It just didn't.

Smith defended each individual's performance to his vice president even when it was clearly human error, assuring his boss that the mistake would not be repeated and admonishing the miscreant not to let it happen again. The workforce, supervisors, and middle managers were a mix of experienced long-term employees and some recent hires. All were qualified for their jobs. Interviews with them evoked similar opinions: they were unlucky; they and their manager were doing all that could be done; maybe the new systems and machinery just couldn't perform to the standards for which they were designed.

Everything came to a head one Friday when a worker Smith had appointed to a responsible position made an error resulting in the destruction of some expensive equipment. Smith was called in by his boss to explain what went wrong. After analyzing and explaining what had happened, he began to defend the employee. His man was first rate, but was having some problems at home; he'd made a mistake, but wouldn't repeat it. Smith intended taking no other action, not even moving the individual into a less responsible position. The vice president had had enough. Smith was immediately relieved of his duties and assigned to staff pending reassignment.

The same afternoon, the vice president asked Bob Cleeter if he would take over the experimental manufacturing unit. Cleeter was also an experienced manufacturing manager; in fact, he and Smith had known each other for years. He'd known that Smith's organization was not performing adequately, but had attended to his own responsibilities and had not followed the situation. Cleeter was briefed on everything that had happened, including why Smith was no longer in charge. Cleeter was given all the reports on previous equipment tests and the rest of the documentation, and given the weekend to prepare to take charge on the Monday. Cleeter knew that change was necessary. The question was what change—what actions should he take to achieve success and turn the organization around?

Cleeter analyzed the breakdown and realized that every single problem could have been overcome by someone taking action to correct the problem before it had progressed to the point of breakdown. In every case, someone had either failed to do something that should have been done or had done something incorrectly.

Cleeter reviewed the training given the unit. On paper, it seemed adequate; however, the facts demonstrated otherwise. He also considered how Smith had led his unit, and concluded that Smith had not been sufficiently demanding of his workers and managers, nor had he done enough to hold them accountable for their mistakes. He allowed them to assume that the failures resulted from bad luck or the system rather than insufficient effort or knowledge. He also realized that two of his managers had not been doing all they could, while others in subordinate positions seemed to be doing more than their fair share.

Positioning theory says the change needed is primarily in the mind of the communication receptors, in this case, those in the failed experimental unit. Cleeter knew what they were thinking:

1. We had a competent, technically qualified and well-liked leader who did his best.

2. We were given the training deemed necessary and were still unable to cope with system problems.

3. We did everything we could.

4. We were either unlucky or the system is bad and cannot be made to work.

Cleeter knew that he had a very difficult positioning problem to overcome. First, he had to position himself as a leader. He could not compete with George as an understanding and likable leader. He had to present himself as much more demanding.

He might reposition later, but only after the unit started performing adequately. At the same time he had to change the unit's mind-set from "unlucky" to "unstoppable."

On Monday morning, his appointment was announced. He first called in the two lax managers and relieved them of their duties. He promoted two of those whose records appeared promising in their place. He called a meeting of the entire organization. He announced the changes he had made, and said that henceforth every worker, supervisor, and manager would be held accountable. Using prepared overheads, he showed them the successful results the system received in tests. He reviewed every breakdown, indicated why it occurred and how it could have been prevented. There would be no additional production runs until they had several days of training. Those who designed and tested the system previously would be brought in to certify that they were ready before they returned to their jobs. Afterwards, all the people in the unit would be fully accountable for their own performance.

Moreover, before every production run, the five managers would be required to brief him in detail about how they would supervise the run, and what they would do to continue operations should an error be made or a breakdown occur. However, it was expected that most problems would be anticipated. The members of the unit were to consider themselves individually unstoppable and to recognize they were responsible for doing everything possible to ensure success. Those who didn't want to be in the unit were to report to Cleeter, who would find them places outside the unit in another part of the company.

Cleeter's authoritative style of leadership was not well received. Still, these were professionals, and they wanted the organization to succeed. They didn't like to fail and decided to give him an opportunity to prove himself. Few asked to be transferred either because they did not want to admit failure or because they were afraid to jeopardize their future opportunities, but those that did were accommodated and given reasonable assignments in accordance with their qualifications.

The training went well, and the staff completed it to become certified. More than a few wanted to be first, and no one wanted to be last. The first production run after training and certification of all members occurred a week later. It went off without a hitch. The attitude and confidence of the unit underwent a dramatic change, just as Cleeter had intended.

The unit never had another major breakdown and became the nucleus for the adoption of the new machinery and system throughout the company. While it was some months before they began to develop a fondness for Bob Cleeter, the people in the unit respected what he had accomplished. As the unit's performance improved, he slowly changed his style and relaxed some of his policies, repositioning himself according to the new situation. There was genuine regret when he was promoted and given a new assignment outside the unit.

Analysis of the Problem and Its Solution

This problem and solution were analyzed using positioning. Therefore, some details that might have influenced the leader's actions one way or another have been omitted, as are the more obvious errors initially made by the company and George Smith.

It is clear that Bob Cleeter immediately positioned himself as leader and sought to reposition the organization from "unlucky" to "unstoppable." Positioning focuses on the minds of those to be persuaded, not the product, service, or anything else.

It may be argued that retraining modified the product. This may be so, but the essential thing is that the retraining got the organization thinking about itself differently. This started with Cleeter's presentation of past results and an analysis of each problem that led to their current situation, which demonstrated why the results achieved were not bad luck, they were poor preparation. This led to his conclusion that their training and determination to succeed was insufficient for the task. The presentation in itself was not the clincher.

It only allowed an opening for the retraining and individual certification that Cleeter knew was necessary.

As a leader, Cleeter realized that he could not position himself as a
"nice guy." George Smith had been that to a fault. Had Cleeter been
the first manufacturing manager, he might have succeeded using "good
guy" positioning if he had done the identical analysis and insisted on
accountability from the start. However, he was not the organization's
first leader and he recognized that he had to position himself as a no-
nonsense, directive leader until the organization turned around.

Positioning's importance to leadership has to do with communication and how other people—workers, subordinate managers,
bosses, and customers—see the leader and the organization relative
to others. This perception results in their willingness to follow a
leader enthusiastically, support the leader's organization, and more.
The objective is to get into their minds and build or change a perception of the leader and of the organization.

The Benefits of Being First

Ries and Trout point out that getting there first is the best and
easiest way to establish a position. They ask their readers to name
the first person to fly solo across the Atlantic, the first to set foot
on the moon, the highest mountain in the world, and similar firsts
and greatests. You probably answered Charles Lindbergh, Neil
Armstrong, and Mount Everest in the Himalayas without breaking
a sweat. They ask next who was the second to fly solo across the
Atlantic, the second to set foot on the moon, and the second highest mountain in the world? Point proved.

That's why Bob Cleeter could have adopted the nice guy position had he been the first manager, but not as the new manager.
The organization would not have accepted a "nice guy" leader
making demands, and he would probably have been unsuccessful in
repositioning and fixing it the organization.

What to Do If You Can't Be First

Cleeter demonstrated that you do not need to be the first to carve out a successful leadership position. In the product world, witness the great success of Avis-Rent-a-Car, whose "We Try Harder" advertising campaign stressed that they were definitely not number one. This implied that they were number two in the rental car business, where Hertz was first. They were actually further down the list when the campaign began. Or consider the 7-Up company, which positioned its product as "the uncola," despite the number of other non-cola soft drinks on the market. Organizations are the same.

Leaders should endeavor to position their organizations as "the best," which can mean different things. To Cleeter's organization, it meant that they were unstoppable.

IBM traces its history back to the late 1880s. Through most of its recent history, it has been known as the largest computer company in the world, with between 300,000 and 400,000 employees. When people think about computer companies, IBM is probably the first to come to mind.

Apple didn't come on the scene until 1976, almost a hundred years later. It has less than 30,000 employees. Yet it has successfully positioned itself as producing the most advanced personal computer products. In 2008, *Fortune* magazine named Apple as one of the most admired American companies.[3] My alma mater, the U.S. Military Academy at West Point, is the oldest of the military academies. It positions itself as the preeminent school for leadership and ethics. Its motto is Duty, Honor, Country. With some humor, graduates of the other U.S. academies repositioned West Point as "two hundred years of tradition unhampered by progress." Or in one case, I heard a newly promoted Air Force general introduced by his boss like this: General _____ came into the Air Force without the benefit of a college education, having graduated from West Point."

The Positioning Procedure

To develop your position or to reposition yourself or your organization, you must start with two vital pieces of information:

- Where are you now?

- Where do you want to be?

It is critical that you be congruent with the position you want to occupy. West Point has graduated proven leaders for two hundred years: Generals Ulysses S. Grant, Robert E. Lee, Douglas MacArthur, Dwight David Eisenhower, George S. Patton, H. Norman Schwarzkopf, and David Petraeus, to name a few. Therefore, the position they have chosen makes sense. Other schools, well known or not, also have positions with which they are congruent and which are readily accepted in the minds of both students and outsiders.

Bob Cleeter had to get his production people retrained and certified. If he didn't have the time or resources to do this, he might not have been able to achieve the new position of "the unstoppable organization."

Drucker wrote that leadership is marketing because he knew that leadership dealt with people and influencing them to achieve their maximum potential. He knew that this could not be accomplished without communication. The concept of positioning is cutting-edge communication technology for the leader.

CHAPTER 23

The Role of Influence and Persuasion on Strategy and Tactics

first encountered the power of influence and persuasion in an assignment at the strategic level of psychological operations during the first Gulf War. Many think psychological operations have to do with dispensing disinformation, that is, lying, cheating, and fabricating propaganda. Actually, a good psychological operation is almost the exact opposite. It needs to be both truthful and credible to be believed and effective. The length to which this is carried can be surprising.

A famous example from World War II had to do with some enterprising psychological operations officer offering a "satisfaction guarantee" to any German noncommissioned or commissioned officer who surrendered voluntarily to American troops. If the new prisoner had second thoughts within a certain period, he would be allowed to return to the enemy. I guess the thinking was that nobody in his right mind would take his captors up on this offer, because, on return, admitting voluntary surrender would mean facing a German firing squad for desertion.

However, one day a German noncom by the name of Fridolin Hopf, who had crossed the lines and surrendered, announced that he was dissatisfied and demanded to be returned to German forces under the terms of this "guarantee." The intelligence chief of the U.S. 6th Armored Corps made the decision to let him go. So they loaded him up with candy, cigarettes, and such and sent him back. They turned him into a propaganda tool that further increased their credibility. "Feldwebel Hopf didn't like it here, but he was our only dissatisfied customer among several hundred. Just ask him. You'll find him in Bunker No. 6, Barracks 4."[1] This demonstrates the importance credibility has in any use of influence and persuasion, even propaganda.

It was the common requirements of successful salesmanship and leadership that first alerted me to a connection between the two. Thus, when I read Drucker's much broader claim that leadership was marketing, the ground was already prepared for me to consider this revolutionary notion.

Although Drucker wrote much on ways to motivate others to high performance and, as noted in earlier chapters, repeatedly advocated that knowledge workers must be led, not managed, he generally ignored both influence and persuasion, probably because he thought they involved the manipulation of those led, which was something he very much opposed. Although there are numerous definitions of both terms, the basic difference between the two is that influence is an act that produces an effect without apparent effort, whereas persuasion requires effort to produce a desired effect. In both cases, an effect is sought. I discuss the two together in this chapter.

Influence and persuasion focus primarily on the tactical implementation of both marketing and leadership, but they affect decisions at the strategic level as well. As leadership tactics, direction and permissiveness are corollaries to influence and persuasion.

A leader who is thinking ahead rather than responding to an immediate problem must first consider the environment in which these alternatives will be implemented at the tactical level, which makes it part of a strategic decision. In decisions about what a post-Saddam Iraq would look like, it was assumed by the Bush administration that Iraq would immediately become a functioning democracy and that victorious U.S. troops would be "greeted as liberators," Vice President Cheney said prior to the war.[2] The administration assumed a model taken from victory over the Axis powers in World War II. However, this assumption completely ignored Iraq's history, religion, and culture. Few outside the administration familiar with the Middle East were surprised at what actually happened.

The principles of influence and persuasion are important at all levels of marketing and at all levels of the marketing model of leadership. However, influence and persuasion are especially important in leading large groups. In this way, they differ from the principles of segmentation.

The Mass Mind

In 1895, Gustave Le Bon published the first study on what he called the "collective or mass mind," *The Crowd: A Study of the Popular Mind*.[3] Although marred by racism and sexism, among other defects, his book is still considered by many academics one of the most influential works on social psychology ever written. It analyzed mass behavior and was said to have affected not only Freud's thinking but also that of Mussolini and Hitler. In addition to crowd behavior, it discussed everything from the characteristics and mental unity of the crowd to its sentiments, morality, reasoning power, and imagination.

Among Le Bon's conclusions:

- When human beings flock, whether by interest, random mob, culture, religion, or country, the interaction of minds results in a collective mind much different from, and not simply a summing of, the total of minds making up the mass.

- This collective mind may respond much differently to stimuli than the ordinary mind would respond to an identical stimulus.

- Different collective minds, depending on the situation and general conditions may not respond identically to the same stimulus.

- The mass mind operates more on emotion than logic.

- The mass mind is contagious—that is, beliefs rapidly pass from one mind to another to result in a common belief.

Some elements of Le Bon's theories, including the idea that that collective minds may not respond identically to the same stimulus if the situation and general conditions differ, are not different from what we have seen in segmentation or our discussions of Drucker's views of motivation. In general, Le Bon's analysis of the "mass mind" is not always as much at odds with segmentation as you might think, since a segmented group may itself constitute a particular mass mind.

Le Bon's theories confirm some of the principles about leading groups discussed earlier: A mass mind may exist, and might respond differently from the mind of each individual who is part of it; and in dealing with it, we must pay much closer attention to the emotions and possibility of contagion than when we lead by treating individuals separately.

Thus, although consideration and treatment of individuals is foremost in a majority of leadership situations, it is never safe to ignore the concept of the mass mind.

Strategies of Influence and Persuasion

What is important is not to master every single strategy of influence and persuasion, but to understand that such strategies exist, that they are a part of the marketing model of leadership, and that, like other aspects of human behavior, while the techniques can be practiced unethically, the leader can also use them in an ethical manner. The following sections address a few of the most common.

Coercion

It would be foolish to ignore coercion as strategy to influence or persuade. In the moment of application, it works. If you have the authority to fire an individual from a job, a threat—even an implied threat—to do that will usually ensure obedience to whatever you desire at that time. The problem is not what happens in the moment, but what happens afterward. A Mafia "Godfather" may gain what he wants by "reasoning together" at the point of a gun. However, even a Mafioso needs to be concerned with what happens later. Similarly, leaders who use coercion to persuade must be concerned with the intended and unintended consequences of this action. Will the coerced continue to obey when not observed? Will the fact of the coercion affect a willing attitude to support the boss and the mission in the future? Will it encourage those coerced to achieve their best?

For these reasons, coercion, although it might be effective in a given instance, should be used only rarely as a way of ensuring obedience and only as a last resort or when time is critical. As I noted in an earlier chapter, "command and control" may give the leader authority to enforce orders, but it is not in and of itself leadership. Yet there are instances where even an undesirable, unsavory method of persuasion may have a positive benefit; for example, to get things done in the short run or when time is short.

Sincerity

I recently heard an instructor at the famous Dale Carnegie Institute relate a story that illustrates the crucial importance of sincerity and its immense power in persuasion and influence.[4] In this speaking course, students are frequently required to give impromptu speeches.

One student told a story about accidentally scattering ash across his lawn, which caused the new grass to turn blue rather than green. He was convinced that this had occurred, and cited various facts supporting it. This incident took place when Carnegie himself was conducting his courses.

During the critique of the speech, Carnegie pointed out that while the speech was interesting and well presented, it was unbelievable because growing blue grass was impossible. Carnegie expected that to end it. No one in the class actually believed that the student had grown blue grass. However, the student didn't give up. He persisted in asserting that he had successfully grown blue grass. Carnegie reminded the student that had ash actually been used to grow blue grass, it would be an immensely valuable technique and the student would become famous. Still the student stuck by his story without wavering, and passionately defended it as the truth, bringing in yet additional verbal "proof" to support his story.

Carnegie was astounded when he noticed that several members of the class began to believe that maybe the student had succeeded in growing blue grass. Carnegie stopped attacking the story and instead asked those who now thought this was possible what had happened to alter their beliefs. All agreed it was the presenter's sincerity that had convinced them; that if anyone was this sincere in his beliefs, there must be some truth to his story, no matter how unlikely.

Carnegie concluded that the power of sincerity to influence and persuade, perhaps only second to coercion, was especially pronounced when the audience's knowledge about the subject was lacking. This illustrates how crucial it is that the leader believe in something before attempting to demonstrate the sincerity required to influence or persuade anyone else. This is as it should be. Recall that Drucker told us that a mission that people could believe in was critical. No one else can believe in any mission you present unless you believe first.

Increasing Commitment

Most salespeople know that it is easier to make a sale if a small commitment toward a sale is gained first, rather than pressing immediately for final purchase. "Just looking" may be expanded to a presentation, discussion, and maybe trial before final purchase. It is human nature not to want to commit to anything all at once, especially if what is desired is unfamiliar, perceived as difficult or dangerous, or seems potentially subject to negative consequences.

Yet, eased into a situation through a series of increasing commitments, many will commit acts they previously would not have entertained. One of the most remarkable instances of this that I not only witnessed but participated in was a three-day "Fear into Power" seminar conducted by motivational guru Tony Robbins.

I had heard about this seminar, which began with a "fire walk" where participants walked a fifteen- to twenty-foot bed of white-hot coals. It was recommended by Dr. Kenneth Blanchard, co-author of *The One Minute Manager*, who had made this fire walk himself. I had heard various theories about how this was possible, among them that it was a physical phenomenon and that walkers could not be burnt. I had also heard that some were seriously injured.

The "fire walk" conducted the first evening was optional, but I wanted to attend the seminar specifically for this experience. I was surprised to find more than a thousand people in attendance. All were required to sign releases whether or not they intended to "walk." Robbins began by repeating that the fire walk was not a required part of the seminar. He asked those who did not intend to perform this act to hold up their hands. I estimated that perhaps 15 percent did this, including a woman and her daughter seated to my immediate left. The woman turned to me and said: "I don't know how you are going to do something like this, or would even want to. We would never do something as dangerous nor as foolish."

Over the next several hours, Robbins guided us through a series of meditations and confidence-building exercises. Then he said,

"Those who are going to do the fire walk, please take off your shoes and socks and leave them here. If you do not intend to do the fire walk, please do the same thing and accompany those who are going to walk to the fire lines as a courtesy to them."

"My God, he's going to get them to walk too," I thought to myself.

Outside about twenty fire lanes were burning with white-hot heat. Whenever one would die down, some of Robbins' assistants would throw some more wood on the coals and the line would flare up again. It definitely got your attention. It took at least an hour for everyone to complete the walk. As interesting as the phenomenon of the fire walk, equally of interest is that virtually everyone who had held up their hands several hours earlier to indicate that they were not going to do the walk, did so anyway. That included the woman and her daughter, "who would never do such a dangerous or foolish thing."

I have seen this many times in many situations. I'm told that a service organization that facilitates bone marrow extraction, a process needed to treat certain types of cancers but painful and uncomfortable to complete, solicits volunteers using the same persuasion technique. The first commitment is simply to receive general information, then to learn more about the extreme need of the recipient, next to witness the procedure, and so on, all of which leads to the commitment to endure the pain and discomfort for the good of the patient. Increasing commitment is a powerful persuasion and influence strategy and an important part of the marketing model of leadership.

Referral, Social Proof, and Conformity

During the height of the hippie years in the early 1970s, a friend and I happened to be on a subway train one Saturday night. At one stop, we picked up a number of college-age students going to Boston. A couple of older women entered the train so my friend and I rose and gave them our seats. As we looked down the length of the car, we saw that the students were all dressed more or less alike albeit in a somewhat haphazard fashion. Virtually every male sported long, unruly hair. At a quick glance, they bore a remarkable resemblance to one another. My friend winked at me and commented, "They are nonconforming." This was extremely insightful. The students were nonconforming to adult society, but, in the midst of nonconforming, they were conforming to their own subculture.

How did this come to be? Since I'm sure that many if not all of these students were from middle- to upper-class families, I'm certain that they did not learn this mode of dress at home. They must have learned it in college. Yet few of their professors dressed this way or looked like this. However, within groups in which there is a dearth of information, individuals tend to refer to others as to what to do. This is not a new phenomenon.

A well-known psychological experiment claims to be intended to rate the attractiveness of a set of individuals based on their photographs. The true purpose is to see to what extent an individual can be influenced to rate someone as particularly attractive based solely on the social proof furnished by others. The psychologist forms a group based on four fake subjects and one real test subject. The group is shown a number of photographs and is asked to select "the most attractive."

All photographs have been pretested to confirm the one in each set actually considered most attractive and least attractive by a large number of participants. In advance, the control group is instructed to select the photograph of the one determined by the pretest to be the least attractive. The group is then presented the first set. Each of the false subjects, one after the other, selects the least attractive in that set and asked to justify the selection. The real subject of course goes last. The process is repeated with some variation with each set. Sure enough, most subjects attempt to agree with the others in the group in their selection.

Individuals frequently refer to others for social proof and conform to what they perceive knowledgeable individuals do. For this reason, game show hosts and others influence applause by having plants in the audience begin clapping or by using laugh machines. Is this unethical? Deceiving those led by the technique used in the supposed selection of the most attractive individual in the photographs is. On the other hand, since knowing that social proof and referral will be sought in a situation in which there is little information available and that there is a human tendency to conform, it is foolish not to be prepared to provide that proof.

Influence and persuasion are major components of the marketing model of leadership. The psychology of human thought and behavior must be understood and practiced as a part of this model.

■ EPILOGUE
Drucker's Legacy

A genius such as Peter Drucker comes along maybe once every hundred years. That Drucker should devote his genius and his entire working lifetime of more than seventy years to thinking about work, and guiding us to be more effective, efficient, productive, and enthusiastic about our work, is our good fortune.

Like other geniuses who do not simply stop thinking and put down the tools of their labor and abandon them, Drucker was passionately devoted to his profession. He tried to continue to work to the very end. With the help of his wife, Doris, and his friends and colleagues, he succeeded to the best of his ability. He did not quit thinking, analyzing, and perfecting his powerful ideas and concepts because he never considered them complete and finished. As he wrote, "Anyone who continues to do what made him successful in the past is doomed to failure." Times change; new technologies are developed.

Many of Drucker's concepts, such as those on influence and persuasion that I attempted to look at in Chapter Twenty-Three, have barely been explored. Other basic notions go on and on. Yet even they must be explored and refined in the context of the present environment. Thus, although Drucker asserts that the basics of leadership haven't changed over the millennia and that Xenophon's book on leadership written two thousand years ago is still the best, not all of Drucker's vision can be applied without first adapting it to present conditions.

Professor Joe Maciariello, Drucker's friend, colleague, and sometime coauthor, told me that he had recently watched Drucker's videos made in the 1960s. He told me how wonderful they were and that they were still useful today in teaching executive students how to manage. However, he said, they had one drawback. The context had changed. The clothing, automobiles, and other devices were fifty years old. Inventions such as computers, cell phones, and pocket electronic calculators didn't exist. This made his teaching sometimes difficult to relate to. Also, some of his ideas only pointed the way.

For this reason, much of Drucker's work on leadership must be continued by others. I hope this book is but the beginning of renewed interest in his ideas and that others will seek to continue his legacy through the further development of his work, especially on leadership—the most important aspect of management.

■ NOTES

Introduction

1. Elizabeth H. Edersheim, *The Definitive Drucker* (New York: McGraw-Hill, 2007), p. 17.
2. Peter F. Drucker, *The Practice of Management* (New York: HarperCollins, 1954), p. 194.
3. Peter F. Drucker, *Management: Tasks, Responsibilities, Practices* (New York: HarperCollins, 1973, 1974), p. 463.
4. Peter F. Drucker, "Leadership: More Doing Than Dash," *Wall Street Journal*, January 6, 1988, p. 1.
5. Frances Hesselbein, Marshall Goldsmith, and Richard Beckhard, *The Leader of the Future* (San Francisco: Jossey-Bass, 1996), p. xi.
6. Drucker, *The Practice of Management*, p. 192.
7. Peter F. Drucker, *Management Challenges for the Twenty-First Century* (New York: HarperBusiness, 1999), p. 21.
8. Drucker, *Management: Tasks, Responsibilities, Practices*, p. 64.
9. Drucker, *Management: Tasks, Responsibilities, Practices*, p. 463.

Part One

1. Peter F. Drucker, *Managing the Nonprofit Organization* (New York: HarperCollins, 1990), p. 9.

Chapter One

1. Peter F. Drucker, *Managing the Nonprofit Organization* (New York: Harper-Collins, 1990), p. 4.
2. Claire Cain Miller, "Glassdoor.com Lists Naughtiest and Nicest C.E.O.'s of 2008," *New York Times* Technology, December 26, 2008; available online at http://bits.blogs.nytimes.com/2008/12/26/which-ceos-were-naughty-and-nice-in-2008/?scp=1&sq=best%20CEOS%20to%20work%20for&st=cse; access date: May 4, 2009.

3. Peter F. Drucker, *Management: Tasks, Responsibilities, Practices* (New York: HarperCollins, 1973, 1974), p. 79.

4. Drucker, *Management: Tasks, Responsibilities, Practices*, pp. 80–86.

5. Gregory Harrington, "Montgomery Ward Catalog to Return," UPI.com, January 14, 2009, accessed at http://www.upi.com/ Business_News/2009/01/14/Montgomery-Ward-catalog-to-return/ UPI-10931231958541/ June 8, 2009.

Chapter Two

1. Peter F. Drucker, *Management: Tasks, Responsibilities, Practices* (New York: HarperCollins, 1973, 1974), p. 125.

2. Drucker, *Management: Tasks, Responsibilities, Practices*, p. 129.

3. John Baker, "Business Plans Are Nothing; Business Planning Is Everything," Country Business, 2008; accessed at www.country-business.com/growyourbiz/ legal_finance/article.aspx?id=6080, May 4, 2009.

4. Drucker, *Management: Tasks, Responsibilities, Practices*, p. 122.

5. Drucker, *Management: Tasks, Responsibilities, Practices*, p. 126.

6. Thomas F. Mulligan and James Flanigan, "Prolific Father of Modern Management," *Los Angeles Times*, Business Section, November 12, 2005, p. A-1; accessed at http://articles.latimes.com/2005/nov/12/business/fi-drucker12, December 26, 2008.

7. Peter F. Drucker, *Managing in a Time of Great Change* (New York: Truman Talley Books, 1995), pp. 39–40.

8. Peter F. Drucker, *On the Profession of Management* (Boston: Harvard Business Publishing, 1998), pp. 51–52.

Chapter Three

1. Peter F. Drucker, *Managing in a Time of Great Change* (New York: Truman Talley Books, 1995), p. 137.

2. Peter F. Drucker, *Managing for the Future* (New York: Truman Talley Books, 1992), p. 253.

Chapter Four

1. Peter F. Drucker, *Managing the Nonprofit Organization* (New York: HarperCollins, 1990).

2. Peter F. Drucker, *On the Profession of Management* (Boston: Harvard Business Press, 1998), pp. 5–17.

3. Peter F. Drucker, *Management Challenges for the Twenty-First Century* (New York: HarperBusiness, 1999), p. 43.

4. Peter F. Drucker, *Managing in Turbulent Times* (New York: HarperCollins, 1980), p. 61.

5. Peter F. Drucker, *Managing for Results* (New York: HarperCollins, 1964), p. 203.

6. William A. Cohen, *A Class with Drucker* (New York: AMACOM, 2008), Chapter 17.

7. William A. Cohen, *The Art of the Strategist* (AMACOM, 2004).

8. B. H. Liddell Hart, *Strategy: Second Revised Edition* (Meridian) (New York: Plume, 1991).

9. J.F.C. Fuller as developed in Anthony John Trythall, *"Boney" Fuller* (New Brunswick, N.J.: Rutgers University Press, 1977), p. 108.

Chapter Five

1. Peter F. Drucker, *Management: Tasks, Responsibilities, Practices* (New York: HarperCollins, 1973, 1974), p. 128.

2. Drucker, *Management: Tasks, Responsibilities, Practices*, pp. 496–498.

3. Drucker, *Management: Tasks, Responsibilities, Practices*, p. 496.

4. For a summary of work on this topic, see "Hawthorne Effect," Wikia Education, accessed at http://psychology.wikia.com/wiki/Hawthorne_effect, December 30, 2008.

5. Drucker, *Management: Tasks, Responsibilities, Practices*, p. 496.

6. Jay Mathews and Peter Katel, "The Cost of Quality," *Newsweek*, September 7, 1992, p. 48.

7. Drucker, *Management: Tasks, Responsibilities, Practices*, p. 497.

8. Drucker, *Management: Tasks, Responsibilities, Practices*, pp. 498–504.

9. Drucker, *Management: Tasks, Responsibilities, Practices*, pp. 504–505.

Part Two

1. Peter F. Drucker, *The Practice of Management* (New York: HarperCollins, 1954), p. 192.

Chapter Six

1. William A. Cohen, *A Class with Drucker* (New York: AMACOM, 2008), p. 114.

2. For a more complete analysis of these struggles, see Michael Schwartz, "Peter Drucker and the Denial of Business Ethics," *Journal of Business Ethics* 17, no. 15 (November 1998), 1685–1693. I disagree with the author that Drucker denied "business ethics." Drucker's definition of what constituted business ethics was different from others' but not nonexistent; in fact, he created his own.

3. Peter F. Drucker, with Joseph A. Maciariello, *The Daily Drucker* (New York: HarperBusiness, 2004), p. 129.

4. Peter F. Drucker, *The Changing World of the Executive* (New York: Truman Talley Books, 1982), pp. 235–237.

5. Kate Galbraith, "A. Carl Kotchian, Lockheed Executive, Dies at 94," nytimes.com, December 22, 2008, accessed at www.nytimes.com/2008/12/23/business/23kotchian.html, June 8, 2009.

6. Drucker, *The Changing World of the Executive*, p. 242.

7. Drucker, *The Changing World of the Executive*, p. 245.

8. Drucker, *The Changing World of the Executive*, p. 245.

9. Drucker, with Maciariello, *The Daily Drucker*, p. 126.

10. Drucker, with Maciariello, *The Daily Drucker*, p. 86.

11. Drucker, with Maciariello, *The Daily Drucker*, p. 86.

12. Drucker, with Maciariello, *The Daily Drucker*, pp. 248–254.

13. Peter F. Drucker, *Management: Tasks, Responsibilities, Practices* (New York: HarperCollins, 1973, 1974), p. 367.

14. See Drucker, *Management: Tasks, Responsibilities, Practices*, pp. 366–375. Although Drucker and others declare this is part of the Hippocratic Oath, this is not true. See Cecil M. Smith, "Origin and Uses of Primum Non Nocere—Above All, Do No Harm!" *Journal of Clinical Pharmacology* 45 (2005): 371–377. I discuss this point further in Chapter Ten.

15. Peter F. Drucker, *Management Challenges for the Twenty-First Century* (New York: HarperBusiness, 1999), pp. 175–176.

Chapter Seven

1. Peter F. Drucker, *Managing the Nonprofit Organization* (New York: Harper-Collins 1990), p. 9.

2. Peter F. Drucker, *Management: Tasks, Responsibilities, Practices* (New York: HarperCollins, 1973, 1974), p. 612.

3. Peter F. Drucker, with Joseph A. Maciariello, *The Daily Drucker* (New York: HarperBusiness, 2004), p. 3.

4. Perry M. Smith, *Taking Charge* (Washington, D.C.: National Defense University, 1986), pp. 28–29.

5. Brigid McMenamin, "Humbled by the Internet," Forbes.com, July 27, 1998, accessed at www.forbes.com/forbes/1998/0727/6202048a.html, May 27, 2008.

6. For more details, see Francis Pisani, "Vets Declare 'War' on CNN," Salon.Com, July 24, 1998, accessed at http://dir.salon.com/story/news/feature/1998/07/24/news, May 27, 2008; and Reed Irvine and Cliff Kincaid, "CNN Eats Crow but Goes Easy on Blame," Media Monitor, July 16, 1998, accessed at www.aim.org/publications/media_monitor/1998/07/16 .htm, May 27, 2008.

7. Perry M. Smith, "CNN: Three Years After Tailwind," Visionary Leadership, Ltd., accessed at http://members.aol.com/genpsmith/tailwind.html, May 27, 2008.

8. Peter F. Drucker, *Management Challenges for the Twenty-First Century* (New York: HarperBusiness, 1999), p. 175.

Chapter Eight

1. "The Seven Deadly Sins," WhiteStoneJournal.com, June 18, 1996, update March 26, 2009, accessed at www.whitestonejournal.com/seven_deadly_ sins/, May 6, 2008.

2. Randy "Duke" Cunningham, Media Release Statement, O'Melveny & Myers LLP, November 28, 2005, accessed at www.signonsandiego.com/ news/politics/cunningham/images/051128cunningham_resign.pdf, June 2, 2008.

3. Peter F. Drucker, "The American CEO," *Wall Street Journal*, December 30, 2004, and June 2, 2008, online edition accessed at http://online.wsj.com/ article/SB113207479262897747.html, June 2, 2008.

4. Kenneth Blanchard and Spencer Blanchard, *The One Minute Manager* (New York: William Morrow, 1982).

5. Jeanne Sahadi, "CEO Pay," CNN: Money, August 20, 2005, accessed at http://money.cnn.com/2005/08/26/news/economy/ceo_pay/ December 3, 2006.

6. John A. Byrne, "The Man Who Invented Management," *Business Week*, November 28, 2005, accessed at http://businessweek.com/magazine/content/05_48/b3961001.htm, June 4, 2008.

Chapter Nine

1. Peter F. Drucker, "The New Meaning of Corporate Social Responsibility," *California Management Review* 26, no. 2 (Winter 1984): pp. 53–63; see p. 56.

2. Drucker, "The New Meaning of Corporate Social Responsibility."

3. "A Brief History of the AFDC Program," n.d., U.S. Department of Health and Human Services, p. 6, accessed at http://aspe.hhs.gov/hsp/AFDC/baseline/1history.pdf, April 16, 2008.

4. Gregory Acs, "Do Welfare Benefits Promote Out-of-Wedlock Childbearing?" in Isabel V. Sawhill, "Welfare Reform: An Analysis of the Issues," Urban Institute, May 1, 1995, accessed at www.urban.org/publications/306620.html#chap11, April 16, 2008.

5. "U.S. Society: Social Welfare," U.S. Mission to Germany, updated January 2009, accessed at http://usa.usembassy.de/society-socialsecurity.htm, May 6, 2009.

6. Drucker, "The New Meaning of Corporate Social Responsibility," p. 62.

7. Ken Burton, "Wal-Mart and the Real Truth About Corporate Values," Social Responsibility Archives, August 8, 2006, accessed at www.nextfiftyyears.com/social_responsibility/, April 16, 2008.

8. William A. Cohen, *A Class with Drucker* (New York: AMACOM, 2008) p. 120.

9. Peter F. Drucker, *Management: Tasks, Responsibilities, Practices* (New York: HarperCollins, 1973, 1974), p. 334.

10. "Origins at Tuskegee Institute," National Trust for Historical Preservation, accessed at www.preservationnation.org/travel-and-sites/sites/southern-region/rosenwald-schools/history/origins-at-tuskegee.html, June 8, 2009.

11. Drucker, "The New Meaning of Corporate Social Responsibility," p. 54.

12. "Diversity Recruitment," NAS Recruitment Communications, 2008, accessed at www.nasrecruitment.com/MicroSites/Diversity/articles/featureD16.html, April 22, 2008.

13. David A. Thomas, "IBM Finds Profits in Diversity," Harvard Business School Working Knowledge, September 27, 2004, accessed at http://hbswk.hbs.edu/item/4389.html, April 22, 2008.

14. Michael E. Porter and Mark R. Kramer, "Strategy and Society," *Harvard Business Review* 84, no. 12 (December 2006): 88.

Chapter Ten

1. "The Hippocratic Oath—Classical Version," translated by Ludwig Edelstein, 1943, PBS- Nova, accessed at www.pbs.org/wgbh/nova/doctors/oath_classical.html, June 5, 2008.

2. Cecil M. Smith, "Origin and Uses of Primum Non Nocere—Above All, Do No Harm!" *Journal of Clinical Pharmacology* 45 (2005): 371–377.

3. Andrew Waterman, "Automobile Emissions and Air Pollution," accessed at www.mbhs.edu/departments/magnet/coursesandlife/RandE/matsci/awtoxicreport.html, June 8, 2009.

4. Peter F. Drucker, *Management: Tasks, Responsibilities, Practices* (New York: HarperCollins, 1973, 1974), pp. 320–322.

5. See Polina Vlasenko, "How Did We Get into This Mess? The Origins of the Housing Crisis," American Institute for Economic Research, September 21, 2008, accessed at www.aier.org/research/commentaries/554-how-did-we-get-into-this-mess-the-origins-of-the-housing-crisis, January 1, 2009; and Edward J. Kirk, "The Subprime Mortgage Crisis," n.d., accessed at www.rli-epg.com/articles/Subprime-Mortgage-Crisis.pdf. June 8, 2009.

Part Three

1. Peter F. Drucker, "Leadership: More Doing Than Dash," *Wall Street Journal*, January 6, 1988, p. 1.

2. Frances Hesselbein and Eric K. Shinseki, *Be, Know, Do: Leadership the Army Way* (San Francisco: Jossey-Bass, 2004), p. xi.

Chapter Eleven

1. Peter F. Drucker, *The Practice of Management* (New York: HarperCollins, 1954), p. 194.

2. Drucker, *The Practice of Management*, p. 194.

3. Xenophon, *The Persian Expedition*, translated by Rex Warner (Baltimore: Penguin Books, 1949), p. 99.

4. Xenophon, *The Persian Expedition*, p. 103.

5. Xenophon, *The Persian Expedition*, p. 124.

6. Xenophon, *The Persian Expedition*, p. 108.

7. Xenophon, *The Persian Expedition*, pp. 282–287.

8. Xenophon, *The Education of Cyrus*, translated by Wayne Ambler (Ithaca, N.Y.: Cornell University Press, 2001), pp. 52–53.

9. Xenophon, *The Education of Cyrus*, pp. 53–54.

10. Xenophon, *The Education of Cyrus*, p. 51.

11. Xenophon, *The Education of Cyrus*, p. 67.

12. See Peter F. Drucker, "Leadership: More Doing Than Dash," *Wall Street Journal*, January 6, 1988, p. 1.

Chapter Twelve

1. Peter F. Drucker, *The Practice of Management* (New York: HarperCollins, 1954), p. 194.

2. Frances Hesselbein, Marshall Goldsmith, and Richard Beckhard, *The Leader of the Future* (San Francisco: Jossey-Bass, 1996), p. xi.

3. Peter F. Drucker, *Managing for the Future* (New York: Truman Talley Books, 1992), p. 336.

4. Office of the Secretary of Defense, Population Representation in the Military Services, 2004, Chapter 4 Sources of Commission, accessed at www.defenselink.mil/prhome/poprep2004/officers/commission.html, June 25, 2008.

5. Peter F. Drucker, *Managing the Nonprofit Organization* (New York: Harper-Collins, 1990), p. 148.

6. Drucker, *Managing the Nonprofit Organization*, p. 148.

7. Drucker, *Managing for the Future*, p. 108.

8. Peter F. Drucker, *Management: Tasks, Responsibilities, Practices* (New York: HarperCollins, 1973, 1974), p. 249.

9. Drucker, *Management: Tasks, Responsibilities, Practices*, p. 210.

10. Drucker, *The Practice of Management*, pp. 246–247.

11. Peter F. Drucker, *The Effective Executive* (New York: Harper-Collins, 1967), pp. 143–144.

12. Drucker, *Managing the Nonprofit Organization*, pp. 147–152.

Chapter Thirteen

1. It should be noted that May Kay Cosmetics, like other sales organizations, can promote salespeople based on quantifiable performance. This is much less difficult than promoting higher-level managers, or leaders of

organizations in which results are relatively difficult to measure. Mary Kay Cosmetics is built on a multi-level marketing concept, so even staffing for sales manager positions can be based on quantifiable data. However, non-sales positions within the company are just like those in any other company insofar as Drucker's views on this aspect of leadership are concerned.

2. Peter F. Drucker, *The Practice of Management* (New York: HarperCollins, 1986) pp. 154–155.

3. Drucker, *The Practice of Management*, pp. 155–156.

4. This section, describing the military system of promotion, is adapted from my book *A Class with Drucker* (New York: AMACOM, 2008), pp. 181–186.

5. Peter F. Drucker, in Frances Hesselbein and Eric K. Shinseki, *Be, Know, Do: Leadership the Army Way* (San Francisco: Jossey-Bass, 2004), dust jacket.

6. Peter F. Drucker, *The Effective Executive* (New York: HarperCollins, 2006), p. 83.

7. Colin Powell, *My American Journey* (New York: Random House, 1995).

8. Peter F. Drucker, *People and Performance* (New York: HarperCollins, 1977), pp. 81–83.

9. Drucker, *The Effective Executive*, pp. 78–92.

10. Peter F. Drucker, *The Frontiers of Management* (New York: Truman Talley Books, 1986), pp. 122–125.

Chapter Fourteen

1. See the testimonial written for Frances Hesselbein and Eric Shinseki's book, *Be, Know, Do*, in the introduction to Part Three, repeated again in Chapter Thirteen.

2. Peter F. Drucker, meeting with the author, November 7, 1997.

3. Douglas MacArthur, *Reminiscences* (New York: McGraw-Hill, 1964), p. 70.

4. William A. Cohen, *The Stuff of Heroes: The Eight Universal Laws of Leadership* (Atlanta: Longstreet Press, 1998). After this book was published, it was on the best-seller list for several weeks.

5. Jim Collins, *Good to Great: Why Some Companies Make the Leap . . . and Others Don't* (New York: HarperBusiness, 2001).

6. Peter F. Drucker, *The Practice of Management* (New York: HarperCollins, 1986), p. 157.

7. Peter F. Drucker, *On the Profession of Management* (Boston: Harvard Business Press, 1998), p. 92.

8. Peter F. Drucker, *Management: Tasks, Responsibilities, Practices* (New York: HarperCollins, 1973, 1974), p. 436.

9. Peter F. Drucker, *Managing the Nonprofit Organization* (New York: Harper-Collins, 1990), p. 7.

10. Drucker, *Managing the Nonprofit Organization*, p. 27.

11. Drucker, *Managing the Nonprofit Organization*, p. 23.

12. Drucker, *The Practice of Management*, p. 13.

Chapter Fifteen

1. Peter F. Drucker, *The Effective Executive* (New York: HarperCollins, 1967), p. 58.

2. Ray Williams, "Seven Deadly Habits of CEOs: Failure Rates Run as High as 70 percent in Some Companies," *National Post*, June 14, 2006, p. 8.

3. Judy Warrick, cited in Walter P. Pidgeon Jr., *The Not-for-Profit CEO* (New York: Wiley, 2004), p. 187.

4. Fred Wilson, "The Human Piece of the Venture Equation," A VC: Musings of a VC in NYC (blog post), August 19, 2008, accessed at www.avc.com/a_vc/2008/08/the-human-piece.html, October 9, 2008.

5. Tiffany Hsu, "CEO Turnover Hits a Record High," *Los Angeles Times*, October 9, 2008, p. C5.

6. When I was promoted to general, I attended a two-week course for new generals. It is the only course of this type designed for new promotes. That this program exists emphasizes the increased responsibilities the individual would face from then on at top management levels. Several speakers at the top levels of the military urged that we not do anything different from what had made us successful. Their warnings were well meant and were probably intended to prevent the newly selected generals from running amok out of delusions of grandeur now that they had "arrived." However, taken literally this advice was almost impossible to follow for reasons pointed out in this chapter.

7. Peter F. Drucker, *Management Challenges for the Twenty-First Century* (New York: HarperBusiness, 1999), p. 19.

8. For a complete discussion of Drucker's views of the Peter Principle, see my book *A Class with Drucker* (New York: AMACOM, 2008), pp. 160–165.

9. See also Drucker, *Management Challenges for the Twenty-First Century*, pp. 162–195, and Cohen, *A Class with Drucker*, pp. 231–245.

10. Jack Beatty, "The Education of Peter Drucker," *Atlantic*, December 15, 2005, accessed at www.theatlantic.com/doc/200512u/peter-drucker, September 17, 2008.

Part Four

1. Peter F. Drucker, *The End of Economic Man* (New York: John Day, 1939).
2. Peter F. Drucker, *The Practice of Management* (New York: HarperCollins, 1954), p. 344.

Chapter Sixteen

1. Ruth Ellen Patton Totten and James Patton Totten, *The Button Box* (Columbia: University of Missouri Press, 2005), p. 75.
2. Douglas McGregor, *The Human Side of Enterprise* (New York: McGraw-Hill, 1960).
3. Peter F. Drucker, *Management: Tasks, Responsibilities, Practices* (New York: HarperCollins, 1973, 1974), p. 231.
4. Drucker, *Management: Tasks, Responsibilities, Practices*, p. 235.
5. Drucker, *Management: Tasks, Responsibilities, Practices*, p. 232.
6. Drucker, *Management: Tasks, Responsibilities, Practices*, p. 233.
7. Peter F. Drucker, *The Age of Discontinuity* (New York: Harper-Collins, 1968), p. 289.
8. Drucker, *Management: Tasks, Responsibilities, Practices*, p. 177.
9. Drucker, *Management: Tasks, Responsibilities, Practices*, p. 195.
10. Drucker never wrote a book entitled "MBO," nor did he try to turn it into a fad or, as the developer, capitalize on it.

Chapter Seventeen

1. Peter F. Drucker, *The Practice of Management* (New York: HarperCollins, 1986), pp. 302–303.
2. William A. Cohen, *A Class with Drucker* (New York: AMACOM, 2008), pp. 160–161.
3. Charles Garfield, *Peak Performers: The New Heroes of American Business* (New York: Avon Books, 1986), p. 26.
4. Donna Fern, "The Lord of Discipline," *Inc.*, November 1985, pp. 82–85, 88, 95.
5. Oberg Industries Fact Sheet, 2009, accessed at www.oberg.com/about/fact-sheet.aspx?WT.svl=1, May 8, 2009.
6. Drucker, *The Practice of Management*, p. 305.
7. Drucker, *The Practice of Management*, pp. 306–307.

8. Drucker, *The Practice of Management*, pp. 307–308.

9. Drucker, *The Practice of Management*, p. 307.

10. Drucker, *The Practice of Management*, p. 310.

Chapter Eighteen

1. Whitney Woodward and Mike Bake, "Surge in New Voters Could Aid Obama," Pantagraph.com, October 10, 2008, accessed at www.pantagraph.com/articles/2008/10/10/news/doc48eef38cd4f27666512033.prt?ref=mobile, October 14, 2008.

2. Peter F. Drucker, "Leadership: More Doing Than Dash," *Wall Street Journal*, January 6, 1988, p. 1.

3. Rich Karlgaard, "Peter Drucker on Leadership," Forbes.com, November 19, 2004, accessed at www.forbes.com/2004/11/19/cz_rk_1119drucker.html, October 14, 2008.

4. Peter F. Drucker, *The Essential Drucker* (New York: HarperBusiness, 2001), p. 269.

5. Tom Geoghegan, "A Step-by-Step Guide to Charisma," BBC News, May 26, 2005, accessed at http://news.bbc.co.uk/2/hi/uk_news/magazine/4579681.stm, October 16, 2008.

6. Ronald E. Riggio, *The Charisma Quotient* (New York: Dodd, Mead, 1987), p. 4.

7. Riggio, *The Charisma Quotient*, pp. 162–163.

8. Geoghegan, "A Step-by-Step Guide to Charisma."

9. Riggio, *The Charisma Quotient*, chapters 2 and 3.

10. Peter F. Drucker, *The Practice of Management* (New York: HarperCollins, 1954), p. 278.

11. Peter F. Drucker, *Managing the Nonprofit Organization* (New York: HarperCollins, 1990), p. 159.

12. Peter F. Drucker, *Management Challenges for the Twenty-First Century* (New York: HarperBusiness, 1999), p. 17.

13. Drucker, *Management Challenges for the Twenty-First Century*, p. 21.

14. Adolph Von Schell, *Battle Leadership* (Columbus, Ga.: Benning Herald, 1933), P. 9.

15. Drucker, *Management Challenges for the Twenty-First Century*, p. 21.

16. Von Schell, *Battle Leadership*, p. 12.

17. Drucker, *Management Challenges for the Twenty-First Century*, pp. 20–21.

18. Lawrence, Alexander, "139," in *The Oxford Book of Military Anecdotes*, edited by Max Hastings, editor (New York: Oxford University Press, 1985), pp. 174–175.

Chapter Nineteen

1. Peter F. Drucker, *Management Challenges for the Twenty-First Century* (New York: HarperBusiness, 1999), pp. 20–21.

2. William A. Cohen, *Secrets of Special Ops Leadership* (New York: AMA-COM, 2006), pp. 8–9.

3. Mary J. Riley, Gilda Schott, and Joanne Schmulnick, "Determining Volunteer Motivations," Volunteer Research and Recommendations (January 19, 2002), accessed at www.msue.msu.edu/objects/content_revision/download.cfm/revision_id.353032/workspace_id.275600/Determining%20Volunteer%20Motivations.pdf/ (www.TinyURL.com/volunteermot), June 9, 2009.

4. E. G. Clary, M. Snyder, R. D. Ridge, J. Copeland, A. A. Stukas, J. Haugen, et al. "Understanding and Assessing the Motivations of Volunteers: A Functional Approach," *Journal of Personality and Social Psychology* 74, no. 6 (1998): 1516–1530.

5. "Colony, Chen, and Andrews: Rank and Mean Scores of Individual Items for All Volunteers," in Steve McCurley and Rick Lynch, *Volunteer Management* (Darien, Ill.: Heritage Arts Publishing, 1996), p. 120.

6. John Naisbitt and Patricia Aburdene, *Reinventing the Corporation* (New York: Warner Books, 1985), pp. 85–86.

7. For example, see Ian Bessell, Brad Dicks, Allen Wysocki, and Karl Kepner, "Understanding Motivation: An Effective Tool for Managers," June 2002, University of Florida IFAS Extension, accessed at http://edis.ifas.ufl.edu/HR017, October 28, 2008.

8. Peter F. Drucker, *Management: Tasks, Responsibilities, Practices* (New York: HarperCollins, 1973, 1974), p. 195.

9. James Moschgat, "A Janitor's Ten Lessons in Leadership," Captain Rosha's Cyberworld, 2008, accessed at www.captrosha.com/a_janitor.htm, October 29, 2008.

10. Angela M. Bowery, "Motivation at Work: A Key Issue in Remuneration," n.d., accessed at www.remuneration.net/motivation_at_work.htm, October 28, 2008.

11. Drucker, *Management Challenges of the Twenty-First Century*, p. 21.

12. Drucker, *Management Challenges of the Twenty-First Century*.

Part Five

1. Peter F. Drucker, *Management: Tasks, Responsibilities, Practices* (New York: HarperCollins, 1973, 1974), p. 463.

2. Drucker, *Management: Tasks, Responsibilities, Practices*, p. 64.

3. Peter F. Drucker, *Management Challenges for the Twenty-First Century* (New York: HarperBusiness, 1999), p. 21.

Chapter Twenty

1. Peter F. Drucker, *Management Challenges for the Twenty-First Century* (New York: HarperBusiness, 1999), p. 21.

2. Robert E. Gunther, "Peter Drucker—The Grandfather of Marketing: An Interview with Dr. Philip Kotler," *Journal of the Academy of Marketing Science*, June 18, 2008, accessed at http://www.springerlink.com/content/841700072588g856/, May 9, 2009.

3. Peter F. Drucker, *The Practice of Management* (New York: HarperCollins, 1954), pp. 37–38.

4. Peter F. Drucker, *Managing the Nonprofit Organization* (New York: Harper-Collins, 1990), pp. 73–84.

5. Peter F. Drucker, *Management: Tasks, Responsibilities, Practices* (New York: HarperCollins, 1973, 1974), p. 63.

6. Drucker, *Management: Tasks, Responsibilities, Practices*, p. 64.

7. Robert E. Wood, quoted in A. D. Chandler Jr., *Strategy and Structure* (Cambridge, Mass.: MIT Press, 1962), p. 235.

8. National Research Council with the collaboration of the Science Service, *Psychology for the Fighting Man*, 2nd ed. (New York: Penguin Books, 1944), p. 307.

9. Wolfgang Luth, "Command of Men in a U-Boat," speech given in 1943 at a German naval officers' course, reported in Harald Busch, *U-Boats at War* (New York: Ballantine Books, 1955), p. 162.

10. For the whole story as I remember Drucker explaining in the classroom, see my book *A Class with Drucker* (New York: AMACOM, 2008), pp. 97–100. For the material as Drucker wrote it, see *Management: Tasks, Responsibilities, Practices*, pp. 62–65.

11. "About AMA: Definition of Marketing," American Marketing Association Web site, October 2007, accessed at www.marketingpower.com/AboutAMA/Pages/DefinitionofMarketing.aspx, November 7, 2008.

12. Al Ries and Jack Trout, *Positioning: The Battle for Your Mind* (New York: McGraw-Hill, 1981).

Chapter Twenty-One

1. See Glenn Kessler, "Obama Clarifies Remarks on Jerusalem," Washington Post.com, June 5, 2008, accessed at http://blog.washingtonpost.com/44/2008/06/05/obama_backtracks_on_jerusalem.html, June 10, 2009, and "Facing Criticism, Obama Modifies Jerusalem Stance," Reuters, June 5, 2008, accessed at www.reuters.com/article/idUSN0547673120080605, June 10, 2009.

2. Don Peppers and Martha Rogers, *The One to One Future* (Currency/Doubleday 1993). The editor of *Inc.* magazine called it "one of the two or three most important business books ever written." Business 2.0 named Martha Rogers one of the nineteen most important business gurus of the past century.

3. Tom Peters and Robert Waterman, *In Search of Excellence* (New York: HarperCollins, 1982).

4. Chester Burger, *The Chief Executive* (Boston: CBI Publishing, 1978), p. 48.

5. Jerome M. Rosow, "A View from the Top," *Success*, February 1986, p. 69.

6. Kenneth Labich and Ani Hadjian, "Is Herb Kelleher America's Best CEO? Behind His Clowning Is a People-Wise Manager Who Wins Where Others Can't," *Fortune*, May 2, 1994, accessed at http://money.cnn.com/magazines/fortune/fortune_archive/1994/05/02/79246/index.htm, May 9, 2009.

7. Suzanne Marta, "Tears, Kisses Mark Herb Kelleher's Send-Off at Southwest Airlines," *Dallas Morning News*, Business Section, June 3, 2008, p. 1.

Chapter Twenty-Two

1. Jack Trout, "'Positioning' Is a Game People Play in Today's Me-Too Market Place," *Industrial Marketing* 54, no. 6 (June 1969): 51–55.

2. Al Ries and Jack Trout, *Positioning: The Battle for Your Mind* (New York: McGraw-Hill, 1981), p. 2.

3. Anne Fisher, "America's Most Admired Companies," *Fortune*, March 17, 2008, pp. 65–67.

Chapter Twenty-Three

1. David Hertz, "The Radio Siege of Lorient," in William E. Daugherty and Morris Janowitz, *A Psychological Warfare Case Book* (Baltimore: John Hopkins Press, 1960), pp. 387–388.

2. Interview with Vice President Dick Cheney, NBC, *Meet the Press*, transcript for March 16, 2003, accessed at www.mtholyoke.edu/acad/intrel/bush/cheneymeetthepress.htm, December 9, 2008.

3. Gustave Le Bon, *The Crowd: A Study of the Popular Mind* (Mineola, N.Y.: Dover Publications, 2002, reprint of English translation published in 1896).

4. Dale Carnegie Training, "Session 6," *Stand and Deliver* (CD) (Niles, Ill.: Nightingales-Conant, 2007).

■ ABOUT THE AUTHOR

William Cohen is president of the Institute of Leader Arts at www. stuffofheroes.com and has spoken and given workshops around the world. Executives and managers from more than fifty countries have heard him speak. He has taught in the graduate schools of California State University Los Angeles, University of Southern California, TUI University, and the Peter Drucker and Masatoshi Ito Graduate School of Management at Claremont Graduate University. He is the author of books translated into eighteen languages, including *A Class with Drucker, The New Art of the Leader, The Stuff of Heroes*, and *The Art of the Strategist*.

Cohen is also a retired major general from the U.S. Air Force Reserve and has previously held executive positions in several companies and was also president of two private universities. In addition to his B.S. in engineering from the U.S. Military Academy at West Point, he has an M.B.A. from the University of Chicago and an M.A. and Ph.D. in management from Claremont Graduate University. He is a distinguished graduate in residence of the Industrial College of the Armed Forces in Washington, D.C.

Cohen's awards include the Outstanding Professor's Award at California State University Los Angeles (1982), the Freedoms Foundation of Valley Forge George Washington Honor Medal for Excellence in Economic Education (1985), and the California State University Los Angeles Statewide Outstanding Professor Award (1996). In 1999, he was named one of four "Great Teachers in Marketing" by the Academy of Marketing Science from nominees from around the world. In 2002 he received an honorary doctorate in humane letters from the International Academy for Integration of Science and Business in Moscow, Russia. Cohen was the

2006 Goolsby Distinguished Visiting Professor in Leadership at the College of Business Administration at the University of Texas at Arlington. He is the recipient of the 2009 Distinguished Alumnus Service Award from Claremont Graduate University. Cohen has served on various city, state, national, corporate, and trade boards and boards of directors.

■ INDEX